To David & Pat
+ Kids !!

Fond regards
Phil & Ruth
Feb 1990

SANTA MONICA

Pictorial Research by Rhonda Bright
"Partners in Progress" by Robert J. Kelly

Produced in cooperation with
the Santa Monica Historical Society

Windsor Publications, Inc.
Chatsworth, California

SANTA MONICA

Jewel of the Sunset Bay

an illustrated history by
Marvin J Wolf and Katherine Mader

**Windsor Publications, Inc.—
History Books Division**
Managing Editor: Karen Story
Design Director: Alexander D'Anca
Photo Director: Susan Wells
Executive Editor: Pamela Schroeder

Staff for *Santa Monica: Jewel of the Sunset Bay*
Manuscript Editors: Amy Adelstein, Jerry Mosher
Photo Editor: Robin Mastrogeorge
Senior Editor, Corporate Biographies:
　Judith L. Hunter
Production Editor, Corporate Biographies:
　Una FitzSimons
Customer Service Manager: Phyllis Feldman-Schroeder
Editorial Assistants: Kim Kievman, Michael
　Nugwynne, Michele Oakley, Kathy B. Peyser, Susan
　Schlanger, Theresa J. Solis
Publisher's Representative, Corporate Biographies:
　Charlie Dresser
Layout Artist, Corporate Biographies: C. L. Murray
Production Assistant: Deena Tucker
Designer: Ellen Ifrah

Library of Congress Cataloging-in-Publication Data
Wolf. Marvin J.
　Santa Monica : Jewel of the Sunset Bay : an illustrated history / Marvin J. Wolf. Katherine Mader : Partners in progress by Robert J. Kelly. —1st ed. p. cm.
　"Produced in cooperation with the Santa Monica Historical Society."
　Bibliography: p. 133
　Includes index.
　ISBN 0-89781-310-3
　1. Santa Monica (Calif.)—History. 2. Santa Monica (Calif.)—Description—Views. 3. Santa Monica (Calif.)—Industries. I. Mader, Katherine. II. Kelly, Robert J. III. Title.
　F869.S547W65 1989
　979.4'93—dc19　　　　　　88-31522
　　　　　　　　　　　　　　　　CIP

©1989 Windsor Publications, Inc.
All rights reserved
Published 1989
Printed in the United States of America
First Edition

Windsor Publications, Inc.
Elliot Martin, Chairman of the Board
James L. Fish III, Chief Operating Officer
Michele Sylvestro, Vice President/Sales-Marketing

RIGHT: *Well-dressed visitors enjoy a Sunday stroll along Santa Monica's beachfront boardwalk in the early 1900s. Courtesy, Santa Monica Historical Society*

FRONTISPIECE: *Photo by Pete Saloutos*

Contents

Acknowledgments	**7**
CHAPTER ONE Shoreline Genesis	**9**
CHAPTER TWO End of the Line	**25**
CHAPTER THREE Fun City	**37**
CHAPTER FOUR More Than the Sum of Its Parts	**53**
CHAPTER FIVE Re-drawing the Map	**73**
CHAPTER SIX The Provinces	**89**
CHAPTER SEVEN Partners in Progress	**99**
For Further Reading	**133**
Index	**134**

To Frank and Cecille Wolf,
and to
Norman, Julia, David Paul, Al,
Isabel, Pauline, Donna, Raquel,
and Ellie—who made it all possible.

Acknowledgments

Any book is an intensely collaborative process; delving into the history of a complex community like Santa Monica would have been virtually impossible without the cooperation of a great many people who offered their time, expertise, and knowledge, quite freely.

We are indebted to the Santa Monica Historical Society, which encouraged this project in ways too numerous to mention, and which opened its archives to provide materials not otherwise available. In particular we are grateful to Mrs. Louise Gabriel, who conceived the title and who was an inexhaustible source of suggestions, many of them helpful.

Linda Sepulveda Eastman, George Bundy, and Angie Marquez Olivera were generous with their time and family lore.

Jim Seal very graciously allowed us unrestricted access to his private collection of regional public transportation history.

Despite very heavy workloads, reference librarians throughout the Santa Monica Public Library system were unfailingly helpful in locating valuable reference material.

Hynda Rudd and Rob Freeman of the Los Angeles City Archive were most helpful in providing access to rare original documents and in suggesting research approaches.

Pam Schroeder and Amy Adelstein, editors at Windsor Publications, provided keen editorial insights and were always available for guidance.

Marvin J. Wolf
Katherine Mader

Santa Monica comes to life as the sun rises over the Pacific Ocean. Photo by Justine Hill

CHAPTER ONE

Shoreline Genesis

Santa Monica's early beachfront development consisted of these simple wooden shacks. This 1890s photo also shows the famous "99 Steps," which connected the beach with the palisades bluff. Courtesy, Santa Monica Historical Society

Living was easy. The sun was warm—but not too warm—rain was limited to a couple of dozen days a year, and winters were mild. And the light! The soft, even glow from the low clouds of early morning and late afternoon . . . the warm, glorious direct rays of the sun falling straight across thousands of miles of placid sea to illuminate late afternoons and early evenings . . . the light was fantastic.

Nature provided in abundance. Pure water gurgled from a multitude of streams and springs. The nearby canyons offered an inexhaustible supply of firewood. Large predators rarely visited the area. The neighbors were peaceable kin.

There were plenty of fish to be easily seined from the ocean; shellfish to be dug from the shallows of the bay; deer, rabbits, and other small game to be had in the mountains; and everywhere, growing wild, plants from which berries, roots, and acorns could be harvested. There were even little pockets of jimsonweed, which when dried could be brewed into a mildly narcotic tea.

The first settlers to arrive in what is now called Santa Monica were no doubt charmed by this early Southern California life-style. Like many later immigrants, they had journeyed far from colder climes. Their ancestors had slipped across the snow and ice and rocky islands of the post-Ice Age Bering Strait—at least 20,000 years ago, maybe more—from Siberia, and after several generations of wandering south, arrived in the area of today's Santa Monica, where they found many reasons to stay.

The women dressed in short cloaks of rabbit fur or deer hide, while the men usually went naked. They created a currency in sea shells, and put up structures on high ground where a creek ran into the ocean, providing fresh water and a quick launching spot for their canoes. These low, airy structures were framed with saplings and covered with rushes from seaside marshes. In the canyons they left little middens of worn-out tools, broken bone fishhooks and needles, the gnawed-over remains of such local cuisine as coyote, skunk, and wildcat, and huge numbers of cracked and broken shell implements. They buried their dead up the coast at a place they named Topanga.

The Gabrieleño Indians made their bowls and cooking containers out of soapstone, which was easy to carve and did not crack when heated. Shell, bone, stone, and wood were also used to make necessary household items, such as baskets, fishhooks, and hunting weapons. Courtesy, Southwest Museum, Los Angeles, California

These were the Indians whose descendants would be called Gabrieleños by the Spanish settlers who eventually replaced them. The two cultures first glimpsed each other on October 9, 1542, when Juan Rodríguez Cabrillo, a Portuguese serving the King of Spain, sailed into Santa Monica Bay.

Cabrillo had been sent by Antonio de Mendoza, first viceroy of New Spain (Mexico) from 1535 to 1549, to find the elusive passage connecting the Pacific and Atlantic oceans. On June 27, 1542, Cabrillo sailed from the port of Navidad, on Mexico's Colima coast, with the 200-ton galleon *San Salvador* and the 100-ton carrack *Victoria*, along with several smaller launches, to explore what was believed to be the "island" of California. Cabrillo took note of the Indians, the palisades, and the placid anchorage provided by Santa Monica Bay before sailing on to a premature death on his flagship in 1543.

More than 200 years went by before Europeans returned. By 1769 the Catholic Church had begun to colonize and proselytize California's Indians by establishing a chain of missions that would eventually run the length of the present state. Gaspar de Por-

LEFT: Bonifacio Marquez, the son of Francisco Marquez who was one of Santa Monica's original landowners, posed for this family portrait with his son Miguel in the late 1800s. Courtesy, Santa Monica Historical Society

FAR LEFT: The Sepulveda adobe, pictured here in 1884, was one of several residences built by Don Francisco Sepulveda and his sons near the San Vicente springs. Built in 1863, the last remnants of this house were finally torn down in 1937. Courtesy, Santa Monica Historical Society

tolá, governor of Lower California, led an expedition north from San Diego toward Monterey Bay, which had been explored by Sebastian Vizcaino in 1602. With Portolá came two Franciscans, Father Juan Crespi and Father Francisco Gomez.

They paused at springs on what is now the site of University High School in West Los Angeles. Certain pious legends first documented in 1822, one from "sierra de Santa Monica" and the other from "parage de Santa Monica," find the inspiration for the naming of the area in these springs. According to one version, Father Crespi and Father Gomez said mass near the springs, and Father Crespi then named the place "Las Lagrimas de Santa Monica." *Lagrimas* are tears, and, as the legend goes, the clear water trickling from hillside ducts inspired Crespi to recall Saint Monica, mother of Augustine, among the most venerated early Christians.

Monica lived in fourth-century Africa, a lady of extraordinary virtue. But one of her sons, Augustine, kept her in tears. He was lazy, would not yield to her teachings, and would not be baptized in the Church. Augustine was carried away by heresy, and led an immoral life.

In despair his weeping mother, Monica, went to the bishop. And wept some more. "Wait," said the bishop. "Continue to pray. The child of so many tears cannot perish." History records that Augustine fell deathly ill, heard his mother's prayers, mended his ways, and embraced the Church. We know him now as Saint Augustine, Bishop of Hippo, and to this day he remains one of the major influences in the Roman Catholic Church.

An equally hoary variation of the naming legend credits two Spanish soldiers, based in 1781 at the new Pueblo de Los Angeles, with discovering the springs and seeing the tears of Santa Monica in its gentle flow.

Whichever version may be closer to the truth, the area around the springs eventually became known as Santa Monica, a vast expanse of grassy plains, wooded canyons, magnificent palisades, and pristine beaches. Except for a few Indians who had pru-

The Marquez family hosted a popular annual "May Day" picnic in Santa Monica Canyon for the area's rancheros. Members of the Marquez, Carrillo, and Reyes families are shown in this group photograph at the 1888 picnic. Courtesy, Santa Monica Historical Society

dently retreated to the more remote canyons, and for smugglers who used the remote beaches to transfer their contraband cargoes, Santa Monica was uninhabited.

In 1821-1822 California passed from being a Spanish possession to become part of the new Republic of Mexico. Around that time, the swelling population of Los Angeles began to eye the vacant lands to the west. When the governor of California, José María Echeandía, proclaimed that citizens who owned at least "150 head of horned cattle" could request grants of public land, Xavier Alvarado and Augustin Machado, pioneer residents of Los Angeles, petitioned to be granted "the place called Santa Monica." Known more colloquially as Boca de Santa Monica, the "mouth of the canyon," it extended north to Topanga and inland a considerable distance. Alcalde, or Mayor, José Carrillo was ordered to give Alvarado and Machado the use of the land.

In 1831 Machado gave his interest in Boca de Santa Monica to Alvarado. Alvarado died soon afterward, and his sons abandoned the grant to Ysidro Reyes and Francisco Marquez. Reyes built an adobe on the rim of the canyon; he later moved in the canyon because coyotes, bobcats, and wolves were carrying off his chickens, lambs, and calves. His son, Ysidro Reyes II, was the first white child born in Santa Monica.

Marquez built his house in the canyon, at the end of what is now Seventh Street. Reyes' and Marquez' descendants still live on portions of those original properties.

The following year, Don Francisco Sepulveda, who was wealthy, influential, and the owner of far more than 150 cattle, was granted rights to "the place called San Vicente y Santa Monica." This rancho included all of present Santa Monica, an area bounded by today's Pico Boulevard and Santa Monica Canyon, running from the sea east to Westwood, and north to the summit of the mountains overlooking the San Fernando Valley. Sepulveda built a ranch house near the spring; he also kept a larger home in Los Angeles.

As neither grant specified boundaries, the grantees disagreed over who actually owned Santa Monica Canyon. In 1839 the new governor, Juan Bautista Alvarado, regranted the tracts to the disputing parties—again without firm boundaries. Sepulveda almost immediately lost the title papers and had to petition for still another grant. In 1846 Governor Pío Pico obliged him. Meanwhile the Pueblo's leading citizens took sides in the dispute. Carrillo, Dominquez, and the Talamantes brothers supported Sepulveda, while the Machado brothers and Lugo took the side of Reyes and Marquez.

The issue was taken to the governor, to lesser officials, and to the courts. Nothing was settled while Mexico ruled California.

Just south of Rancho San Vicente y Santa Monica was La Ballona, a rancho comprising today's Ocean Park, Venice, Palms, much of Culver City, and the wetlands of Ballona Creek. In 1839 Governor Alvarado had granted it to co-grantees Augustin Machado and his brother Ignacio, and the brothers Tomás and Felipe Talamantes.

One theory derives the name La Ballona from "La Ballena," meaning "the whale." However, the Talamentes family has a tradition that the rancho was named for the city of Bayona in northern Spain, with a change in spelling.

The Machados were prominent in regional affairs. Augustin had married Ramona, daughter of Francisco Sepulveda; though illiterate, he served for a time as the Los Angeles alcalde.

Widely respected for his integrity, he once boarded a ship owned by the merchant José Antonia Aguirre, a family legend recounts, to buy dry goods. It was customary for such rancheros as Machado to make their purchases on credit, the bill to be settled in a few weeks or months. After selecting his purchases, Machado was about to have them put in a launch. But the cargomaster, who didn't know Machado, demanded he sign a note.

Machado was astonished. No one had ever demanded such a thing from him, nor from any of his peers. Finally he realized that the cargomaster didn't trust him. Plucking a single hair from his beard, he handed it to the man with such serious demeanor that nobody could mistake his motives. "Deliver this hair to Señor Aguirre; say it is from the beard of Augustin Machado. It is my guarantee of payment, and will fulfill your responsibilities to Aguirre." Much abashed, the cargomaster carefully placed the hair in his books.

The ranchos were isolated and remote. On horseback it took most of a day to reach Los Angeles; by oxcart it could take three or four days, especially if the ground was muddy.

In an account written in 1913, Herminia Reyes, a granddaughter of Ysidro Reyes born in 1856, explained how the ox teams traveled. Indians walked ahead with long poles to scare up any cattle that lay in the path. The carts, called *carretas*, had large wooden wheels and a pole at each corner. If women and children rode, a canopy was stretched across for shade.

From the poles hung a *cangelon*, or cow horn, filled with soap, periodically applied to the wooden axles to prevent their burning from the constant friction. If the soap ran out, someone would cut a cactus and smear the pulp on.

Reyes recalled that her cart once ran out of soap and there was no cactus. Her grandmother told the Indian driver to use some rice pudding they had brought along. "The Indian would throw a spoonful of pudding on the wheel and one in his mouth and say, 'It is a shame to feed pudding to a wheel.'"

These first residents of the Santa Monica Canyon area lived simply in adobe huts which featured packed clay floors, whitewashed walls, and roofs of tar or tule, a variety of bullrush. Their days, which began at sunup and ended not long after dark, were filled with toil. Each year was a pastoral cycle of flocks and herds being shifted from plain to valley according to the season. There was an annual roundup for branding and selection for breeding or slaughter; a time for shearing sheep and for tanning hides; and a season for rendering tallow and for planting and harvesting grain.

There were few diversions, no traveling shows nor theaters. When people wanted to relax, to swap news and rumors, or to blow off a little steam, they found a reason for a gathering or a fiesta—a wedding, birthday, baptism, the celebration of a holy day, even a funeral, and invited all their neighbors.

These parties often lasted for days and included dancing and singing, races, and games. A favorite entertainment for younger men involved burying a rooster up to its neck in sand or loose dirt and then trying to pluck the bird from the ground—while hanging from a horse running full tilt.

The favored sport was horse racing; none were more enthusiastic than the Sepulveda and Pico families, between which an intense rivalry had grown. In 1840, for example, a dispute arose over payment of a stake lost by teenaged Fernando Sepulveda to the slightly older Andreas Pico. Don Francisco, citing certain irregularities in the race, refused to pay his son's debt. Alcalde José Lugo ordered him to pay; Sepulveda obeyed but appealed first to the court and then to the governor. Eventually Lugo was overruled, and ordered to repay Sepulveda. He refused, earning himself the eternal enmity of the Sepulveda clan.

The most famous horse race of the era took place in 1852. José Sepulveda, Francisco's son, had bought "Black Swan," an Australian thoroughbred mare, for the unheard-of sum of $10,000. He then challenged the Picos' stallion to a race of three leagues, or about nine miles. Thousands of people came from as far away as San Diego and Monterey for the event.

In a grueling race where supporters were allowed to ride beside the racing animals and whip them, Black Swan won by a few lengths. Sepulveda was said to have collected almost $50,000 in wagers. He rewarded the mare by allowing it to run free on his pastures for the rest of its life.

In 1848 the Mexican-American War was ended by the Treaty of Guadalupe Hidalgo; for the next two years California was ruled by military governors. On September 9, 1850, California was admitted to the Union as the 31st state. One of the first legal actions taken was establishment of a Board of

This baptism performed in Santa Monica Canyon by the St. Augustine by-the-Sea Episcopal Church was cause for a celebration. Courtesy, Santa Monica Historical Society

Lower Santa Monica Canyon, shown here in the 1870s, was a popular site for early tourists and beachgoers. Courtesy, Ed Tynan Photo Collection

Land Commissioners.

After 1851, when the first petitions for confirmation of rancho grants were being filed, this body ruled on the Reyes-Marquez and Sepulveda dispute. To Sepulveda went 30,259 acres of the 58,409 he had claimed. To the Reyes and Marquez heirs went 6,656 acres, and to the Machados, who had previously bought out the Talamantes, 13,919 acres of Rancho La Ballona was granted. U.S. Government patents record the exact descriptions and boundaries of these grants as not finally fixed until 1873 (La Ballona), 1881 (San Vicente y Santa Monica), and 1882 (Boca de Santa Monica).

None of the original grantees lived to see this resolution, and by that time an era had passed. Southern California was becoming increasingly urbanized, and the rural life-style enjoyed by those who controlled the vast land grants was coming to an end. A few years after the courts had finally confirmed the ranchos' boundaries, the heirs of the old rancheros began to encounter two of the most persistent Southern California phenomena, real estate developers and tourists.

From the late 1860s, Santa Monica Canyon and its nearby beaches became a mecca for campers and beachgoers. The Marquez and Reyes families, like many of the rancheros, were very tolerant of such visitors and allowed them unhindered access.

On weekends and long summer days the beaches swarmed with picnickers and sunbathers. In the sycamores of the lower canyons tents were erected. Campers sang and danced far into the evening around blazing bonfires. Others prospected for gold along a quartzite shelf exposed by the low tide; adventure was all they found. In the early 1870s an early entrepreneur rented out a small skiff he had brought from San Pedro for rides through the surf.

To accommodate these early visitors, the Marquez family opened a grocery store in the canyon, its first merchant establishment. It sold staples like cornmeal, coffee, bacon, and lard. Later a two-story, frame building with eight rooms was built near the canyon mouth, a hotel that boasted a dining room and accommodations for 40, dormitory style.

During this period some enterprising souls built a little wharf known as Shoo Fly Landing near the foot of what is now Colorado Avenue. It connected to a trail that ran eastward through the mesa pastures to

One of Santa Monica's most popular natural wonders was the Arch Rock, shown here circa 1890, which was so wide that during low tide horse-drawn wagons could pass through its opening. During high tide, however, the road was impassable. Arch Rock seemingly vanished overnight in 1906; since conflicting stories have been reported regarding its fate, the mystery behind the Arch's disappearance remains unsolved. Courtesy, Santa Monica Historical Society

the Hancock Ranch, just outside Los Angeles. Bubbling to the surface of the Hancock area were, and still are, huge tar pits now known as the La Brea area (*Brea* is Spanish for "tar.") The tar was collected into barrels, loaded on ox-drawn wagons, and hauled to the wharf. Small coastal vessels transported the tar to San Francisco, which was enjoying a building boom in the wake of the Gold Rush.

Colonel Robert S. Baker was a 49er, one of the horde of gold seekers, adventurers, and businesspeople who flocked to California after the discovery of gold in 1848. A Rhode Islander by birth, he became wealthy by selling mining supplies through his company, Cooke & Baker, which was based in San Francisco. Later, with his friend, Edward Fitzgerald Beale, he went into the sheep ranching business.

In 1872 Baker paid a visit to the tar-shipping wharf. Looking out over the rolling, grassy mesas, he envisioned a sheep ranch. All he had to do was buy the land.

The heirs of Don Francisco Sepulveda, primarily his son José Dolores, land wealthy and cash poor, had increasingly focused their social and business attentions on the growing city of Los Angeles. Baker bargained hard and came away with the entire Rancho San Vicente y Santa Monica for just under $55,000. Soon afterward he negotiated with the Marquez and Reyes families and bought about 2,000 acres of their Rancho Boca de Santa Monica holdings, including Santa Monica Canyon and what is now Pacific Palisades. He then went west to see the Machados, who agreed to part with 160 acres of Rancho La Ballona.

Baker's holdings now included all of the present area of Santa Monica and a small portion of Marina del Rey. All together these lands offered everything required for an excellent ranch, including mountain streams, year-round springs, more than a mile and a half of beaches, a deep-water harbor, sheltered lower canyons, and rolling plains generously endowed with grass.

The consolidated acquisition also made an ideal site for a new city. The record is vague on whether Baker had development

in mind when he started buying land. But less than a year later, now established in Los Angeles, he was joined by his friend and sometime partner, Edward Fitzgerald Beale.

Beale, one of California's earliest and most accomplished land promoters, once served as a federal surveyor. His subsequent success in attracting buyers from the East to properties he acquired inspired Abraham Lincoln to remark that "Beale . . . had become monarch of all he surveyed."

When Beale arrived in Los Angeles in December 1873, the *Express* carried a story asserting he was accompanied by an "eastern capitalist who contemplates the purchase of the San Vicente Ranch" and who planned to build a wharf at Shoo Fly Landing, as well as a railroad connecting it with Los Angeles. But the Easterner, if there was one, apparently changed his mind.

Meanwhile Colonel Baker had not been

Colonel Robert S. Baker came to Santa Monica in 1872 to expand his successful Northern California cattle and sheep ranching business. He promptly bought Rancho San Vicente y Santa Monica for just under $55,000 from the Sepulveda family, and stayed to develop the townsite of Santa Monica with his partner, Senator John P. Jones. Courtesy, Santa Monica Historical Society

The Santa Monica Hotel was originally established as a rooming house for the John P. Jones wharf workers, as depicted here in 1878. This building eventually became the city's first major hotel, and included a Ferris wheel among its attractions. Mrs. Georgina Jones and her three daughters lived at the hotel while waiting for the Miramar to be completed. Courtesy, The Getty Center for the History of Art and the Humanities, Los Angeles, California

Arcadia Bandini Stearns de Baker, pictured here in her later years, was the daughter of Juan Bandini, from one of the wealthiest of Southern California's great founding Spanish families. The widow of landowner Don Abel Stearns, Arcadia married Colonel Robert S. Baker in 1875, giving her new husband influence over the Puente and Laguna ranchos. Courtesy, Santa Monica Historical Society

idle. He courted and married, in 1875, the widow of Don Abel Stearns, the bilingual businessman who had been among the first Americans to settle in Los Angeles. Arcadia Bandini de Stearns was more than a beauty. She was heiress to Stearns' considerable mercantile fortune and to vast land tracts and other holdings inherited from her father, Juan Bandini, among the wealthiest of the early Californians. Though Arcadia's holdings remained her own property, through this marriage Baker gained influence over the Laguna and Puente ranchos.

By now Santa Monica Canyon boasted two hotels, Morongo House and the Seaside Hotel, and both stayed full of frolicking guests. Sometimes, on warm summer days, it seemed like all of Los Angeles was at the beach.

So, few were surprised when the newspapers announced that Baker had associated himself with Beale and "several wealthy Englishmen" and that they were contemplating the creation of an "embryo" metropolis. The plan included wharves, a rail line, an ambitious seaside hotel complex, and a townsite. The new town would be known as Truxton, in honor of Truxton Beale, Edward Beale's son.

It never happened. Instead, Nevada Senator John P. Jones, a multimillionaire through his silver and gold mining interests in Virginia City, Nevada, and Inyo County, California, turned up with bundles of cash and a firm plan to subdivide and develop a new town called Santa Monica.

Jones paid Baker $162,500 for 75 percent of Baker's properties. Together they drew up plans for a townsite bounded by the bay on the west, 26th Street on the east, Railroad Avenue (now Colorado) on the south, and Montana Avenue on the north. On July 10, 1875, the map was recorded in Los Angeles County. Santa Monica was officially a town.

Five days later more than 2,000 people, including some 150 who had steamered down from San Francisco, gathered on the naked plain for an auction of city lots. It was a day of blinding sun, without even a tree for shade. Dust filled the air, stirred by the milling crowd, their horses, and by hundreds of buggies and wagons. Former congressman Tom Fitch, the master of ceremo-

Sunset Trail, shown here in the early 1900s, provided easy access from the palisades to Santa Monica's beachfront. The fenced footpath, which led down the hill and through a tunnel to the beach, was opened to the public until slide damage blocked the tunnel in 1955. Courtesy, Elliott Welsh

nies, was more than equal to the occasion.

Renowned as California's foremost orator, he went on at great length about the unrivaled virtues of Santa Monica:

On Wednesday afternoon at one o'clock we will sell at public outcry to the highest bidder, the Pacific Ocean, draped with a sky of scarlet and gold; we will sell a bay filled with white-winged ships; we will sell a southern horizon, rimmed with a choice collection of purple mountains, carved in castles and turrets and domes; we will sell a frostless, bracing, yet inlanguid air, braided in and in with sunshine and odored with the breath of flowers. The purchaser of this job lot of climate and scenery will be presented with a deed to a piece of land 50 by 100 feet, known as 'lot A, in block 251.' The title to the land will be guaranteed by the present owner. The title to the ocean, the sunset, the hills and the clouds, the breath of the life-giving ozone and the song of the birds is guaranteed by the beneficient God who bestowed them in all their beauty and affluence upon block 251, and attached them thereto by almighty warrant as an incorruptible hereditament to run with the land forever.

He laid it on thick indeed, because Jones had promised to sell him 20 percent of the

Nevada Senator John Percival Jones, a multimillionaire from silver and gold mining, came to Southern California in the 1870s with the notion to build a railroad to transport supplies back to his mines. He stayed to help establish the city of Santa Monica with Colonel Robert S. Baker, buying 75 percent of Baker's properties for $162,000 in 1875. Courtesy, Santa Monica Historical Society

Founding Families

THE JONES FAMILY

John Percival Jones was born in England and came to Ohio as an infant. At the age of 20 he set out for the California gold fields; sailing around Cape Horn, he led a mutiny when the captain refused to feed passengers.

Jones served as sheriff of Trinity County from 1861 to 1864; from 1863 to 1868 he was a member of the California legislature. Then, in 1870, he relocated to Virginia City, Nevada, where he invested heavily in the Crown Point Mine. Crown Point became one of the richest of the Comstock Lode workings—and Jones became a multimillionaire. First elected to the U.S. Senate in 1872, he served five consecutive terms. A spellbinding orator, he counted among his legislative successes efforts to halt Chinese immigration and the prevention of the use of federal troops to guarantee black voter registration in the South.

With Colonel Robert S. Baker, Jones developed a town plan for Santa Monica. In 1888 he built a magnificent home, Miramar, at Nevada (now Wilshire Boulevard) and Ocean avenues, although his official residence remained in Nevada. As a developer he spent one million dollars in Southern California, much of it on the Los Angeles & Independence Railroad, which he hoped would turn Santa Monica into Southern California's premier commercial city.

In 1887 Jones and Mrs. Arcadia de Baker, the colonel's widow, deeded 300 acres near what is now Sawtelle and Wilshire to the federal government for the site of a home for disabled military veterans. To the city they later donated the property for the park at Lincoln and Wilshire, innumerable church and public school sites, the beautiful median strip on San Vicente Boulevard from 26th Street to Ocean Avenue, and the magnificent strip along Ocean Avenue, Palisades Park.

THE VAWTER FAMILY

In 1875 Williamson D. Vawter opened the town's first general store, lumberyard, and planing mill. In 1887 he built the first streetcar line. With his sons he organized First National Bank of Santa Monica. He also helped found the First Presbyterian Church.

William S. Vawter, eldest son of Williamson, was closely tied to his father's businesses. With his father and brother, Edwin James (E.J.) Vawter, he bought 100 acres of Rancho Lucas in 1884, an area later subdivided and developed into the Ocean Park district; with E.J. he started the Santa Monica Commercial Com-

Miramar, the splendid home of Senator John P. Jones, seen here circa 1900, became the popular Miramar Hotel. The three-story Victorian mansion, built in 1888, sported 17 bedrooms and six bathrooms. It was remodeled and enlarged in the mid-1920s and stands today as the Miramar Sheraton Hotel on Wilshire Boulevard near Palisades Park. Courtesy, Santa Monica Historical Society

The Jones sisters and their basketball squad posed on the lawn of Miramar in this 1893 photograph. Marion Jones is seen holding the basketball, with sister Georgina to her left. The game had recently been invented in 1891 by James Naismith of Springfield, Massachusetts. At first women played in their corsets, but later abandoned them due to their constricting nature. Courtesy, Miramar Sheraton Hotel

Members of the Carrillo family played crucial roles in the development of early Santa Monica. Pedro C. Carrillo, pictured here, was the father of Juan Carrillo, and fought in the Mexican War. He went on to marry Josefa Bandini, the sister of Arcadia Bandini Stearns de Baker. Courtesy, Santa Monica Historical Society

pany in 1894. William S. Vawter was a director of First National Bank and later Merchant's National Bank and served for a time as city postmaster. Later he became active in state government and on the board of education.

E.J. Vawter was also an active partner in the family's many enterprises. He served as president of City Water Company in 1896 and as cashier of First National Bank until 1893. As an entrepreneur he established a fresh flower industry, and also started First National Bank of Ocean Park in 1905.

THE CARRILLO FAMILY

The Carrillos are among the oldest families in California; patriarch José Raymundo Carrillo came to California as a soldier in 1769.

His son, Carlos Antonio, was a member of the Mexican Congress. A book, reproduced from a speech by Carlos, was the first printed by a native Californian. In 1837 he was appointed governor of California and was instrumental in having Los Angeles, for a short period, named as the state capital.

In 1847 Pedro C. Carrillo, son of Carlos, guided a messenger from Commodore Robert F. Stockton to General John C. Frémont through enemy-held territory during the Mexican War. Pedro's wife, Josefa Bandini Carrillo, sister of Arcadia Bandini Stearns de Baker, sewed the first American flag raised in Southern California.

Pedro's son Juan served as Los Angeles city marshal from 1878 to 1882. Juan moved to Santa Monica in 1881, where he acted as agent for the Baker family's many interests. In 1884 he acquired the deed to Woodlawn Cemetery, which his heirs officially donated to the city in 1907. In 1888 Juan became a city trustee, serving until 1900. From 1890 to 1897 he was president of the board of trustees and honorary mayor; as such he led a successful fight against locating a Los Angeles city sewage outfall in Venice. From 1904 to 1906 Juan Carrillo served as superintendent of streets. One of his 13 children, Leopold (Leo), would achieve fame as a stage and film actor.

THE MARQUEZ FAMILY

Angie Marquez Olivera, a descendant of Francisco Marquez, the owner of Rancho Boca de Santa Monica, still lives in Santa Monica Canyon. At a New Year's Eve family party in 1916, 13 members of the family became violently ill from botulism poisoning after eating home-canned pears. They were treated by Dr. Hromadka, but only one of them survived.

The victims, including the patriarch Pascual Marquez, are buried in a family cemetery on San Lorenzo, which is not open to the public. Others in the cemetery include relatives and friends, among them Sam Carson, son of famed frontier scout Kit Carson.

THE BUNDY FAMILY

The Bundys, descendants of British Quakers who came to New England in 1636, settled in Santa Monica in April 1876, living initially at Fifth and Ocean Park. George Bundy, who was born in 1906, is a former city manager and was twice elected to the Board of Education. Bundy recalls that as a boy he used to roam the vacant land east of 26th Street. His family had a livery stable where Robinson's department store is now, at 103 Santa Monica Place.

In 1905, his uncle, C.L. Bundy, subdivided 800 acres near what is now San Vicente Boulevard, Wilshire Boulevard, Bundy Drive, and 26th Street, bought from John P. Jones and Arcadia de Baker's Santa Monica Land and Water Company. There were no steam shovels, "so they had to move the earth by hand and with horse-drawn wagons. The route along what's now called Bundy Drive was up a dry creek bed, so they followed the contours of the creek bed to avoid having to move more earth. That's why it's so crooked," he recalls.

Developer Frank Bundy built this private summer cottage on Santa Monica's beachfront, near the California Incline. His wife, Hallie, and his son, Douglas, are pictured here on the front porch in the late 1800s. Courtesy, Santa Monica Land and Water Company Archives

Bathing beauties attracted prospective buyers to a Schader Real Estate promotion for Santa Monica beachfront property in 1907. Courtesy, Santa Monica Historical Society

A team of horses, an elaborately decorated wagon, and a group of musicians were used to entice prospective buyers to a Santa Monica land auction on August 24, 1887. Five-cent, round-trip train rides to the auction site were cleverly advertised on the horse blankets. Courtesy, Ed Tynan Photo Collection

> ## Locations
>
> **Palisades Park,** overlooking Santa Monica Bay, runs along the west side of Ocean Boulevard, from Santa Monica Pier to Santa Monica Canyon. The portion between Montana and Colorado avenues, originally known as Linda Vista Park, was donated by John P. Jones and Arcadia Bandini de Baker, while the portion from Montana Avenue to the canyon rim was donated by the Santa Monica Land and Water Company, founded and owned by Jones and Baker.
>
> **Bronze bust of Arcadia Bandini de Baker,** sculpted by Masahito Sanae, graces the rose garden in Palisades Park, at Ocean and Palisades avenues. It was a joint gift by the Santa Monica Historical Society, the City of Santa Monica, and the Bandini family.
>
> **Statue of Saint Monica** is found in Palisades Park, on Ocean Avenue at Wilshire Boulevard. Created for the 1934 Federal Arts Project by sculptor Eugene Morahan, the statue commemorates the city's namesake.
>
> **Camera Obscura,** built by James P. Jones' brother Robert F. Jones in 1889 on the North Beach, was moved to Palisades Park around 1902. On open exhibition to the public, the device is a rare example of the technology which preceded the invention, in the mid-1800s, of the modern photographic camera.
>
> **Founders Tree** is located on the grounds of the Miramar Sheraton Hotel, at Ocean and Wilshire boulevards. The huge Moreton Bay fig tree was planted by Senator Jones' family between 1879 and 1889.

entire ranch for $47,000, that sum to be paid from the proceeds of the very lots he was selling.

No matter his motivations. It was exactly what everybody had come to hear. The first lots, at the corner of Ocean and Utah (now Broadway), went to Harris Newmark, patriarch of Southern California's leading Jewish family. He bought five lots for $300 each. Auctioneer E.W. Noyes assured him he could have as many more as he wanted at the same price.

By the end of the day more than $40,000 had been taken in. The next day was even better: $43,000. The boom went on for months; people arrived from all over the country. A contemporary newspaper account describes one young collegian from the East who had come to California with $700 intended for his support until he recovered his health. Instead he found an "easy" job tending sheep for $10 a month and invested the $700 in townsite lots. "By the end of the year they'll be worth $7,000," he declared.

History does not record if this young man's optimism was entirely justified, but scarcely nine months after the auction Santa Monica boasted 1,000 people, 150 houses, 75 tents, a church, school district, library, wharf, reservoir for water piped from San Vicente Springs, bathhouse, hotel, and newspaper, the *Outlook*.

There was even a railroad, with track laid as far as Los Angeles. Santa Monica was on its way, and the Los Angeles & Independence Railroad, by linking the Bay City with the rest of the nation, was going to make it Southern California's premier port.

TOP LEFT: *Camera Obscura, located near the North Beach Bath House, provided an opportunity for discreet people-watching for only 10 cents. This beach amusement, built by Robert F. Jones in 1889, relocated to Palisades Park around 1902 and can still be seen at the Santa Monica Senior Center. Courtesy, Santa Monica Historical Society*

CHAPTER TWO

End of the Line

Residents of Santa Monica gathered to welcome the city's first electric streetcar, which began service from Los Angeles to their beach community in 1896. The car pictured here was part of the original Pasadena & Pacific railway, which became the Los Angeles Pacific in 1898. Courtesy, Elliott Welsh

If Santa Monica were to reach its full potential—as believed by Senator John P. Jones, Colonel Robert S. Baker, and the most influential among the merchants, bankers, movers, and shakers who invested in the new town's future—it would be as a great funnel for Southern California. Through the port they envisioned in Santa Monica Bay would pour the merchandise, material, and immigrants needed to develop the entire region.

Half a century earlier the first railroads had rapidly transformed the Eastern Seaboard from wilderness to civilization as farm and factory products became available to distant markets. Baker and Jones believed the West had even greater potential for growth—but only if it could attract new settlers to fuel the expansion of commerce.

California's rail link to the East was a single line, the Central Pacific, terminating in San Francisco, by far the West's largest city. Passengers and cargo bound for Los Angeles were transferred to steamers and

Horse-drawn wagons were able to haul freight up the California Incline, pictured here circa 1915, after the cliffs were scaled back to make way for the construction of a dirt road. Courtesy, Santa Monica Historical Society

shipped south. Those who sought the benefits of immigration and trade for Santa Monica saw that their priorities were to create a suitable port and then railroads to move passengers and goods inland.

San Diego offered a fine port, but it was more than 100 railroadless miles distant. Santa Monica Bay, while deep enough to anchor the largest ships of the era and not given to silting, is not a natural harbor. Most of the year its waters are calm, but there is nothing to shelter vessels from the open sea during winter storms. Nevertheless, from the 1830s, vessels had anchored in Santa Monica Bay's deep water, transferring cargo ashore in small boats to Shoo Fly Landing, near what is now Colorado Avenue.

With a suitable wharf and a breakwater, the promoters thought, Santa Monica Bay could become a magnificent port serving all of Southern California north of San Diego. Such a port would inevitably create enormous demand for waterfront and railhead real estate, thousands of jobs and hundreds of businesses, and immediate population growth for Santa Monica. As Jones and Baker saw it, the port was the key to Santa Monica's future.

The only problem was San Pedro. No more protected than Santa Monica, it could hold vessels drawing up to only 17 feet of water. Moreover, hydrographic engineers advised that a breakwater would invite silting, and thus as a year-round port it would require constant dredging. But San Pedro was the region's established terminus; since the late eighteenth century, ships had lightered goods and passengers there onto Timm's Landing. Angelenos, including many of the city's most powerful and influential citizens, had real estate and other interests to protect in San Pedro.

Since 1851 Phineas Banning had run a stage and wagon line from Wilmington, in San Pedro's inner harbor, to Los Angeles. In 1869 he and others formed the Los Angeles & San Pedro Railroad Company, which built a standard gauge railroad between these points. The City of Los Angeles helped raise construction money by buying Los Angeles & San Pedro Railroad bonds, becoming, in effect, Banning's silent partner in the line.

The Los Angeles & San Pedro became even more important to Los Angeles in 1872 when the Southern Pacific Railroad (SP) announced its intent to bypass the city as it laid new track between San Francisco and Yuma, Arizona. Including Los Angeles would require an additional 150 miles of track; the SP could see little reason to spend money to do so.

The Los Angeles establishment was horrified. A railroad would haul Southern California beef and produce to Eastern markets and return with newcomers to buy real estate. The railroad meant prosperity; if it bypassed Los Angeles, the city would soon wither and die.

There was only one thing to do. Hats in hands, a blue-ribbon Angeleno delegation approached the SP, which was owned by the same foursome who controlled the Central Pacific. What would it take, asked the Angelenos, to bring the railroad to Los Angeles?

Leland Stanford, Mark Hopkins, Charles Crocker, and Collis P. Huntington were not yet known for their charity. They demanded as much as they believed the city could bear, and in the end they got it. The City of Los Angeles gave the SP $600,000, a right-of-way 25 feet wide through the city, 60 acres of land for a depot, and—over the Banning family's objections—the Los Angeles & San Pedro Railroad.

Thus the SP gained control of virtually all shipping into and out of Southern California. Collis Huntington concentrated on squeezing every nickel he could out of the San Pedro & Los Angeles Railroad. With no competition, he immediately raised shipping and passenger rates to nearly unbearable levels.

In February 1875, however, Jones, Baker, and several other notables raised $4 million and began construction of the first leg of the Los Angeles & Independence Railroad. Colonel Joseph Crawford, an engineer, served as general manager. In May 1875 they built a 1,740-foot wharf at Shoo Fly Landing. Eighty feet wide, it was first used to bring in rails, ties, and heavy equipment to build the rail line.

The plan was to link Santa Monica with Los Angeles. Later the line would be extended to Independence, in Inyo County, near Jones' Panamint mines. Eventually the rail would run through Salt Lake City and continue on to connect with the Central Pacific.

In early September a sidewheel steamer offloaded the first steam engine, some flat cars, and gondolas. On October 17, 1875, the first train completed a run from Shoo Fly Landing to a terminal near San Pedro and Fourth streets in Los Angeles. On December 5, 1875, the Los Angeles & Independence delivered its first excursion of 400 sightseers and potential real estate investors to Santa Monica.

In response Huntington immediately cut rates between San Pedro and Los Angeles by 50 percent. The public cheered; clearly competition had its benefits.

Jones was not alarmed. Fabulously rich

This circa 1890 view of the Southern Pacific depot in Santa Monica shows the rebuilt Santa Monica Hotel (right), which was relocated from the bluffs, and the local field which was host to many bicycle races and football games. This same site is the approximate location for today's Sears store near Fourth Street and Colorado Avenue. Courtesy, Santa Monica Historical Society

An 1875 San Francisco newspaper advertisement for the first sale of Santa Monica lots boasted a main commercial harbor for the proposed bay city. Hundreds of prospective buyers from San Francisco arrived by ocean steamer to bid on commercial and residential land. Courtesy, Santa Monica Historical Society

from his mining investments and a power in the U.S. Senate, he was content to wait for his profits. In the interval he announced his intentions to "ruin Wilmington" by blocking federal appropriations for dredging or enlarging San Pedro harbor. Santa Monica, he proclaimed, "was the logical metropolitan center" of Southern California. Los Angeles would never be more than its suburb.

Thus began a struggle which would last nearly 30 years. The first to suffer the consequences were passengers from San Francisco, who could never be sure in advance if their ship would dock in San Pedro or in Santa Monica. Ships' captains made their choices based on allegiance to Jones or Huntington, or to current freight rates. Those meeting arriving passengers were often inconvenienced, since land travel between the rival ports consumed a day.

Huntington kept cutting rates, and by May 1876 twice as many ships and three times as much cargo moved through Wilmington. In September the SP completed its tracks into Los Angeles, allowing shippers to send goods through Wilmington and on to other points in Southern California.

The Los Angeles & Independence track ended in central Los Angeles; Jones couldn't compete. As business dwindled on the railroad, service was cut back. Those in Los Angeles who might have bought summer or weekend homes in Santa Monica could no longer be sure of a reliable commute. Santa Monica's first real estate boom ended with a sigh.

In 1876 several banks failed; financial depression swept the state. A number of Jones' investments went sour, including the Panamint mines. Strapped for cash, Jones ordered a halt to surveying and construction for extending his railroad. In early 1877

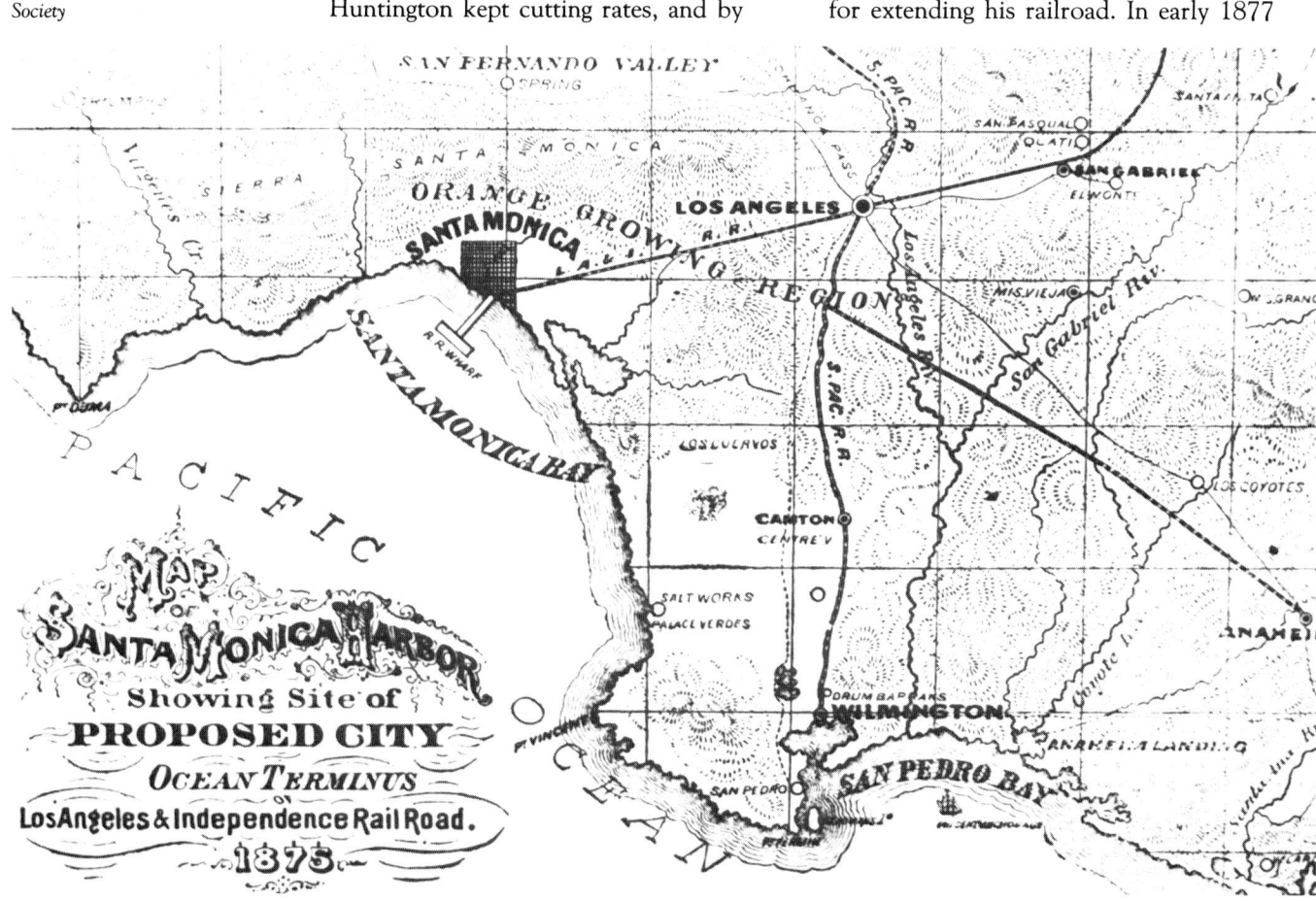

Jones and his partners offered the railroad to Los Angeles County for one million dollars, the cost of the completed construction. But even the county feared the SP. Jones approached the Union Pacific, but Huntington had already spread the word that Jones' line was a poor investment.

The stage was set for Huntington to buy the Los Angeles & Independence for whatever he chose to offer. Jones, now in serious difficulties, seemed glad to accept $250,000.

The transaction closed on June 4, 1877. Huntington's first act was to raise rates on the Los Angeles-to-San Pedro route well above what he had charged before the Los Angeles & Independence tracks to the SP's River station were completed. Two trains a day ran to Santa Monica, with an extra on Sunday.

In September 1878 the *Senator* became the last steamer to dock at the Santa Monica wharf. Soon afterward, SP engineers declared the wharf unsafe because teredos, or shipworms, had eaten virtually through the pilings. Repairs would be too costly, said the SP's engineers. In January 1879 workers began to dismantle the wharf. Despite the "worm damage" the pilings resisted destruction and ultimately had to be sawed off at the waterline at low tide. Wharf lumber washed up on beaches for weeks afterward. Few signs of worms were noted.

The wharf's demise sent Santa Monica into decline. Population fell to 350. Property values evaporated. The *Outlook* suspended publication. Weekend and summer vacationers still flocked to the beaches, but the town's future seemed dim.

By the early 1880s the SP was charging more to move a ton of cargo from San Pedro to Los Angeles than it charged to move the same ton from San Pedro to Hong Kong.

This inequity—and the potential profits it offered to a competitor—did not go unnoticed. In 1887 the Atchison, Topeka & Santa Fe (AT&SF) completed a transcontinental railroad in Los Angeles and then sought an ocean terminal. Moses Wicks, a land developer who controlled some of the Rancho La Ballona waterfront property, which he named Port Ballona, made a deal with the AT&SF to build a harbor in Ballona Lagoon (now Marina del Rey). Plans were drawn and a branch line constructed. The deal fizzled when the land boom collapsed.

But in 1889 the Redondo Railway Company sprang into being with a wharf at Redondo and a narrow gauge rail spur to Los Angeles. Redondo, blessed with a deep underwater canyon, enabled large ships to dock at a short pier. Since these ships would have had to anchor far out in San Pedro with lighter cargoes, Redondo became an almost immediate success. The AT&SF built an extension south from its inactive Ballona Lagoon line, and soon vast quantities of goods were flowing inland through Redondo.

At about the same time, control of Rattlesnake Island, in San Pedro's inner harbor, passed to the Terminal Land Company and was renamed Terminal Island. This company was affiliated with the Los Angeles Terminal Railroad, which built a line from Los Angeles in 1891. The SP's stranglehold on Southern California's shipping was slipping. Collis Huntington quietly began scheming for a new harbor—at Santa Monica.

In 1890 Huntington suddenly replaced Leland Stanford, long a San Pedro advocate, as SP president. Huntington bought half of Jones' Santa Monica holdings, secretly acquired more through agents, and applied for a wharf franchise. He also bought some Pacific Palisades holdings through an agent.

About this time Congress appointed a War Department panel to select a deep water port between Point Dume and San Juan Capistrano; in December 1891 they recommended San Pedro.

Meanwhile Huntington continued to expand his interests in Santa Monica, purchasing a right-of-way on the beach fronting

A Southern Pacific train emerges from the tunnel under Ocean Avenue on its way to the Long Wharf in the late 1800s. These tracks were later replaced by a dirt road called Roosevelt Highway, and the tunnel was eventually enlarged for the modern Pacific Coast Highway. The landmark Arcadia Hotel is visible in the distance. Courtesy, Santa Monica Historical Society

Santa Monica Canyon. Then came the announcement: SP would build a huge port complex just north of Santa Monica Canyon. A wharf would extend almost a mile into Santa Monica Bay. In January 1892 construction began with a 331-foot tunnel under Ocean Avenue and Colorado Avenue. Simultaneously, a trestle was built out from Santa Monica Canyon and tracks were laid to connect the Long Wharf with Santa Monica Depot.

In February 1892 Huntington was able to stymie a U.S. Senate Commerce Committee's $250,000 appropriation to begin work on a port at San Pedro. Congress appointed another panel, the Craighill Board, to reevaluate all sites. Huntington, hedging his bet, continued to expand the SP's San Pedro pier complex.

While the Craighill Board deliberated, Huntington pressed on with construction in Santa Monica. Pile drivers began work on July 26. By September the wharf extended more than 1,000 feet into the bay, and Huntington began wooing public support by conducting tours for Los Angeles officials and businessmen. The highlight of the tour was the dizzying experience of a train ride far out to sea, accompanied by a persuasive SP narration outlining the complex's bright future.

In December 1892 the Craighill Board recommended San Pedro. Undeterred, Huntington pressed on to complete the Long Wharf. In April 1893 he christened it Port Los Angeles, a public relations device to enlist support among influential Angelenos as well as a way to call attention to Los Angeles' proximity to the sea, a fact few Easterners seemed to know.

Almost immediately, the Treasury Department named Port Los Angeles as a sub-port of entry to the Los Angeles Customs District and appointed a deputy to collect duties. That allowed Port Los Angeles to accept cargoes from foreign countries, an important boost to the port's status.

Port Los Angeles thus entered service on May 11, 1893, with the arrival of the collier *San Mateo,* a British-registered vessel owned by an SP subsidiary. Construction continued; on July 14, 1893, the last spike connecting the wharf to SP tracks was driven. A depot opened to the public in October.

Meanwhile, Huntington relentlessly beat the drum to sway public opinion. Nevertheless, the Los Angeles Chamber of Commerce enlisted great numbers of Southern California business and civic organizations to support San Pedro. An appropriation to begin work at San Pedro remained bottled up in the Senate Commerce Committee only because of Senator Jones' influence.

Huntington therefore paid a surprise visit to the Los Angeles Chamber of Commerce, where he harangued startled officials about the virtues of Santa Monica Bay. He then invited Chamber directors to visit the Long Wharf on his private train, afterward treating them to refreshments at the Arcadia Hotel.

Huntington next took his battle to the newspapers, and soon the issue was hotly debated in front-page editorials. Only the *Los Angeles Times* was in favor of San Pedro; the *Los Angeles Express* and the *Herald*, as well as the *Santa Monica Outlook*, favored Santa Monica. (Later the *Herald* changed ownership and switched its support to San Pedro.)

Finally, in April 1894, the Los Angeles Chamber of Commerce met to vote on the issue. Santa Monica lost by a margin of more than two to one; a number of ardent Santa Monica supporters had switched

Coal from Vancouver Island, destined for Southern California, was shipped to the Long Wharf in the 1890s to be used as fuel for the Southern Pacific steam-powered locomotives. Courtesy, Ed Tynan Photo Collection

Newly built Port Los Angeles is pictured here in the mid-1890s, as a Southern Pacific train rounds the bend of the Long Wharf tracks. The port's roundhouse, which was used for the housing and switching of locomotives, is visible to the left. Courtesy, Santa Monica Historical Society

The first steamer to arrive at Port Los Angeles was the San Mateo, *pictured here on that historic day on May 11, 1893. More than 1,000 Santa Monica residents rode in train cars (right) to the pier to welcome this group of travelers and to celebrate this exciting event. Courtesy, Santa Monica Historical Society*

Pictured here in 1912, the Long Wharf was located just up the coast from Santa Monica Canyon and served the early Los Angeles shipping industry when it opened in 1893. When Santa Monica lost the fight to become the area's commercial port in 1908, service to the Long Wharf was discontinued and the tracks and facilities were eventually dismantled. Courtesy, Santa Monica Historical Society

sides. In June, Huntington struck back by asking Congress to appropriate $4 million to build a breakwater in Santa Monica Bay. Construction would be facilitated by using the Long Wharf to haul hundreds of tons of rock out to deep water.

Now, for the first time, the entire nation got involved as newspapers around the country trumpeted the issue. It was noted that Huntington, Jones, and Arcadia Bandini de Baker, Colonel Baker's widow, controlled virtually all of the real estate in and around Santa Monica. The AT&SF Railroad, faced with giving up its share of Southern California freight, supported San Pedro.

After a third panel, the Walker Board, again chose San Pedro in June 1896 over President Grover Cleveland's veto, Congress appropriated $392,000 for San Pedro's inner harbor. The War Department was to supervise construction.

The indefatigable Huntington, though, was not yet through. Secretary of War Russell Alger, a good friend, stalled on the construction of the harbor. Not until April 16, 1899, was the first stone fit into the San Pedro breakwater.

It was thus the beginning of the end for the Long Wharf. Merchants gradually shifted their business to San Pedro. Collis Huntington died on August 13, 1900; SP's new president was Charles Hays. He was succeeded in 1902 by Edward H. Harriman, who controlled the Union Pacific and several other railroads. Pressed by a myriad of other problems, Harriman viewed the Long

Wharf, which required constant maintenance, as a liability.

In 1908 SP discontinued rail service to the wharf and leased it instead to the Los Angeles Pacific, an electric railway system. In the same year, Port Los Angeles was removed from the schedules of the Pacific Coast Steamship Company. In 1910 the port closed forever.

Then, between 1911 and 1920, a series of landslides near Santa Monica Canyon covered the tracks near the Long Wharf. Thus in 1913 the depot building and the outer 1,600 feet of wharf were dismantled; the remaining tracks and facilities, mostly bunkhouses which had passed to the Pacific Electric Railroad, were unceremoniously salvaged or abandoned.

Electric trolleys had come to Southern California in the 1890s. The grand opening of the first electric railway line from Los Angeles to Santa Monica, the Pasadena & Pacific (P&P), founded by Arizona State Militia General Moses H. Sherman and his brother-in-law, Eli P. Clark, took place on April 1, 1896; the route followed present-day Sunset and Santa Monica boulevards. Later that year, service was extended south to Ocean Park. Renamed the Los Angeles Pacific (LAP) in 1898, in 1900 the line was extended to central Hollywood, in 1902 to Playa del Rey, and in 1903 to Redondo Beach.

By 1907 Sherman and Clark had sold 51 percent control of the LAP to the SP, which invested substantial sums in converting the lines from narrow to standard gauge and planning a rapid-transit subway west from downtown Los Angeles. Sherman and Clark sold their remaining LAP stock to the SP in 1910.

That same year, Henry Huntington sold his Southern California interurban interests, including the Pacific Electric (PE), to the SP. Reorganized in 1911, the new Pacific Electric—a consolidation of the LAP, "old" PE, and other SP-owned electric lines—brought service to the Soldiers Home, now the Veterans Hospital. Over the next decade the PE continued to extend track and service to communities throughout Southern California. The modern freeway system virtually replicates the route of the PE at the height of its activity.

A Southern Pacific locomotive which just completed a 22-minute speed record from Los Angeles to Santa Monica skidded off its tracks and onto the lawn of the Arcadia Hotel in 1908. Any farther and the train might have gone over the edge of the bluffs. Courtesy, Santa Monica Historical Society

For those visiting Santa Monica's rapidly growing beach resorts and entertainment and amusement centers, the double-track main lines along Santa Monica and Venice boulevards, the latter especially, known as the Venice Short Line, became the preferred mode of travel; also popular was the old, single-track Los Angeles & Independence line, electrified between 1908 and 1912 and known, for its smooth, rapid service, as the Air Line. Tens of thousands rode these lines on weekends, and many who worked in hot, dusty Los Angeles were encouraged to purchase homes in Santa Monica.

Then, in the 1930s, Southern California's love affair with the automobile turned hot and heavy. In a remarkably short time this spelled the end of the line for the trolleys, known as the "Big Red Cars." Auto traffic became so heavy that trolleys on surface

ABOVE: A Bay City Transit driver proudly stands with his bus in front of the Soldiers Home circa 1924. In nice weather the canvas windows could be removed for open-air comfort. Bay City Transit, formed in 1921, was bought out by the Santa Monica Municipal Bus Line in 1951. Courtesy, Santa Monica Municipal Bus Line

TOP: The Los Angeles Pacific trolley line, which originally began service under the name of Pasadena & Pacific in 1896, consolidated into the Pacific Electric Railway in 1911. One of Los Angeles Pacific's trolley cars is shown here around the turn of the century at one of its many stops. Courtesy, Santa Monica Historical Society

TOP RIGHT: Santa Monica's first roller coaster was built in 1887 and ran from the Arcadia Hotel, at the top of the bluff, all the way into town. The ride lasted one minute and cost a mere five cents. Courtesy, Santa Monica Historical Society

streets often ran far behind schedule. The number of passengers declined, and during the Great Depression the Pacific Electric began switching to bus service, which required only a driver instead of both a conductor and a motorman, and which could offer more frequent trips with fewer passengers. Even so, despite such adjustments, the Pacific Electric's annual operating losses continued to mount.

World War II gasoline and tire rationing, as well as the interruption of new car manufacture, brought a brief reprieve, however. Hundreds of thousands of new arrivals to Southern California used the trolleys to commute to jobs in wartime aircraft factories. Eventually, though, the postwar boom, the largest in regional history, would bring affluence and with it a relentless increase in automobile ownership. By the end of the 1940s the Big Red Cars were doomed.

Pacific Electric replaced its rail passenger service from Los Angeles to Santa Monica via Venice Boulevard with buses in September 1950, leaving only the Air Line with electric rail passenger service to Santa Monica. The Air Line's last run took place on September 30, 1953. Overhead wires were removed; the tracks were used by the

SP for freight trains until March 11, 1988, when the last diesel locomotive pulled out of Fisher Lumber, at Colorado and 14th. Then, claiming that revenues from the line fell short of the $1.5 million required to modernize and renovate the tracks, the SP obtained the permission of the Interstate Commerce Commission to end service, over objections from Fisher Lumber and several Santa Monica groups.

The tracks remain, however, while their replacement, the freeways, are daily clogged with millions of automobiles. Thus Santa Monicans are again seeking ways to reduce commute time to Los Angeles. Under active consideration is a light rail system along the old right-of-way.

Light rail, however, will cost hundreds of millions of dollars—too much for a small city alone to raise. Funding must thus come from federal, state, and county appropriations. Many Los Angeles business and government leaders prefer building a subway, already under construction, to connect downtown Los Angeles with other parts of the city. As this history goes to press, both sides are lobbying the government to fund their respective projects. At stake, say many, is Santa Monica's future.

Locations

The Arcadia Hotel, completed in 1887 and once the finest seaside hotel in Southern California, was located at 1661 Appian Way. It was here that Collis Huntington wined and dined the directors of the Los Angeles Chamber of Commerce while he tried (unsuccessfully) to convince them to favor development of Santa Monica Bay over San Pedro. All that remains of the hotel today are two bricks from the original foundation, which are noted by markers at either end of the present structure.

Robert E. McClure Tunnel, under Ocean Avenue, is now a conduit linking the Santa Monica Freeway (I-10) to Pacific Coast Highway. The tunnel, named in 1970 for the former *Evening Outlook* publisher and state highway commissioner, was dug in 1892 to bring SP tracks to the Long Wharf. Rail use of the tunnel was discontinued in the early 1930s; later that decade the tunnel was enlarged to its present size for highway use.

Fisher Lumber Yard stands at the corner of 14th Street and Colorado Avenue. On March 11, 1988, the last train to use the railbed, constructed originally in 1875 by Senator John P. Jones' Los Angeles & Independence Railroad, departed for the final run to Los Angeles, thus ending 113 years of continuous service.

Soldiers Home trolley station, found in the Veterans Administration complex at Wilshire and Federal avenues, is listed on the National Register of Historic Places. The station once served Vawter's Nevada Avenue (now Wilshire Boulevard) horse car line, until the line was purchased by Sherman and Clark in 1895 and became part of the P&P-LAP. The station remains much as it was at the turn of the century.

Woodlawn Cemetery, located at 1847 14th Street, was established circa 1870 as a family cemetery by the Carrillo family. Its original nine acres were officially transferred to the city by Juan Carrillo's heirs in 1907, and the cemetery has since been expanded to 28 acres. Found here are the graves of many of Santa Monica's pioneer families, including the Machados, Higueras, Lugos, and Talamantes, as well as the Vawter family and Abbot Kinney, founder of Venice. Also on the grounds are an ornate mausoleum, built in 1928, and a monument to the unknown military dead of the Civil War.

CHAPTER THREE

Fun City

In hindsight, the failure of Collis Huntington's grand plans for a marine mercantile mecca was the best thing that could have happened for Santa Monica. Generations of residents of the city by the bay have enjoyed a quality of life which ultimately could never have coexisted with the serious but grimy business of international shipping.

Instead of elbowing its way onto world maps through the rough and tumble of commerce, Santa Monicans swam, strolled, and danced gaily onto the pages of atlases. Campers had enjoyed Santa Monica Canyon's delights since the mid-1800s, when the Marquez and Reyes families welcomed overnight visitors on their property. By the 1880s the town was a favorite seasonal resort; a decade later, beach trolley parties became the rage of Southern California's summers. In January 1890 the *Outlook* estimated that the SP and the Los Angeles & Independence had together carried 250,000 visitors to the beaches during the previous year, in addition to the thousands who

The magnificent Deauville, built in the 1920s on the site of the old North Beach Bath House, was inspired by the famous club in Deauville, France. Featuring a French-medieval exterior, this exclusive family beach club featured a private glass-covered beach, a double-decker esplanade, and an overhead bridge extending from the club to the beach. It was bought out by the Los Angeles Athletic Club in 1927, and was eventually torn down in 1964 after sustaining damage in a fire. Courtesy, Santa Monica Historical Society

37

A stocking-clad swimsuit model beckons local Santa Monica sunbathers in this early 1920s beachwear advertisement. Courtesy, Santa Monica Historical Society

Carrillo family members and their guests competed in the old Spanish game of Spearing Rings in front of the North Beach Bath House in 1912. Judge Juan Carrillo is astride the white horse in the center, Leo Carrillo is on the far left, and Frank Machado is situated to the left wearing a white shirt. Courtesy, Santa Monica Historical Society

arrived in "private conveyances."

Besides bathing beaches, the community offered horseback riding, camping, and picnicking in Rustic and Mandeville canyons and along the shores of Ballona Lagoon, as well as in Santa Monica. Boating, fishing, and duck hunting drew still more visitors. After the turn of the century, the arrival of Panama steamers unloading cargoes of exotic fruits, wildlife, and plants drew great crowds. In the 1870s and 1880s, thousands of weekend sightseers watched Ring Tournaments, vivid displays of horsemanship in medieval costumes, and so-called Spanish Games, which combined elements of the traditional Mexican fiesta with colorful spectator sports from California's Mexican era.

Among Santa Monica's first organizations was the Bonitas, a baseball club founded in 1875. Then as the community grew it offered a great panoply of outdoor sports: auto and cycle racing, tennis, polo, golf, deep sea fishing—even dove hunting, which was then called "pigeon shooting."

The Santa Monica Improvement Club, a lawn tennis association, was founded in 1887 by Abbot Kinney, Colonel Robert S. Baker, Senator John P. Jones, and several other notables. In August 1887 the first tournament, for beginners, pitted locals against entrants from Pasadena, San Gabriel, Pomona, Riverside, and Los Angeles. For many years afterward the Southern California Lawn Tennis Association held annual tournaments at Santa Monica's Casino courts on Third Street.

From these courts came tennis champions who for decades dominated the game in North America and Europe. Among them were Marion Jones, daughter of the senator and a national champion; May Sutton, who took Wimbledon in 1904 and 1907 and who continued to play in tournaments through her 83rd year; Elizabeth "Bunny" Ryan, 18-time Wimbledon winner; Johnnie Doeg, two-time U.S. national champion; Ted Olewine, U.S. national junior boys champion; and glamorous Gertrude "Gorgeous Gussie" Moran, the doubles champion who scandalized Wimbledon by revolutionizing women's tennis togs.

Meanwhile, between 1909 and 1917 Santa Monica was home to the Vanderbilt Cup and Grand Prize, nationally famous auto races which were held along a triangle formed by Wilshire Boulevard, Ocean Avenue, and San Vicente Boulevard.

Polo was also popular in Santa Monica, one of the first communities in the state with its own pitch. The first matches in the area were played in the 1880s in what is now Lincoln Park. About 1926 the sport experienced a revival, stimulated by members of the exclusive Uplifters Club, whose matches attracted internationally noted horsemen and such celebrities as Will Rogers. In 1932 the Riviera Polo Club was used as the equestrian venue for the Olympic Games, and later it hosted equestrian matches between Mexico and an all-California team. Both clubs were located in Santa Monica Canyon.

The community's reputation as a sporting town was not without its darker side, however. By the turn of the century Santa Monica had 3,057 residents and dozens of saloons. These watering holes attracted

When the Chips Were Down

In the 1930s much of Southern California was wide open to illicit enterprise, including prostitution, loan sharking, bootlegging—and gambling. Santa Monica was no exception; at one time there were 15 legal draw poker casinos and innumerable bingo parlors. In addition, bookie joints and illegal gaming casinos flourished underground; the *Outlook* was full of stories detailing raids on restaurants and private homes.

The community's most conspicuous gambling establishment was not in town, however, but riding the waves of Santa Monica Bay. The *Rex*, a luxurious barge manned by 150 croupiers, dealers, bouncers, and bartenders, began operations on May 1, 1938, from its anchorage just over three miles from Santa Monica Beach. Hundreds of patrons were shuttled to the *Rex* on water taxis from Santa Monica Pier to try their luck at faro, 21, poker, roulette, the wheel of fortune, slot machines, and the Chinese lottery.

According to the *Rex*'s master, former bootlegger "Admiral" Tony Cornero, it was all completely legal, because the barge was outside California's jurisdiction. California Attorney General (later California Governor and then Chief Justice of the Supreme Court) Earl Warren was of another opinion. After a court ruled that California's western boundary was formed by a line drawn from Point Dume to Point Vicente, Cornero withdrew to deeper water.

But the *Rex*'s customers were uncomfortable in the rougher waters, and business dropped off. So the following summer Cornero returned, bringing two more gambling ships. Warren responded with a raid by 250 sheriff's deputies, cutting off water taxi service and boarding two of the gambling ships.

Nevertheless, Cornero refused to surrender the *Rex*. While 600 gaming patrons were held hostage, dozens of his minions prowled the decks with tommy guns, while he turned high pressure water hoses on the circling police boats.

The "hostages" were allowed to leave after 12 hours, but the Battle of Santa Monica Bay went on for nine days, until the *Rex* ran out of food and fresh water. Then Cornero decided he "needed a haircut" and went ashore to continue the battle in a courtroom.

He lost, to the relief of Santa Monica's PTA and church groups. After World War II, though, the irascible Cornero tried again, off Long Beach, but authorities soon put him out of business. He then took his action to Las Vegas, where he bought the Stardust Hotel. There, years later, after an argument with a croupier, Cornero suffered a heart attack and died on a craps table.

From 1909 to 1917, racing buffs cheered their favorite drivers in the Vanderbuilt Cup and the American Grand Prize auto races along the triangular route formed by Ocean Avenue, Wilshire, and San Vicente boulevards. Spectators are pictured here in front of the Miramar Hotel during "The Great Race of 1914," with the judges and press situated along Palisades Park. Courtesy, Miramar Sheraton Hotel

Guests of the Miramar Beach Club enjoy a day of socializing and sun in the 1920s. Courtesy, Elliott Welsh

Santa Monica's first movie studio, Vitagraph, filmed about one Western a week after its establishment in 1910 behind the old city hall. Called "the MGM of the early American cinema," the studio helped develop the careers of Rudolph Valentino, Charlie Chaplin, and Mary Pickford. The Rapp Saloon, a beer hall built in 1875, can be seen to the left. Courtesy, Santa Monica Historical Society

attracted hundreds of often rowdy drinkers, especially around the first of the month when pensioners at the nearby Soldiers Home received their stipends.

The saloons—and those who patronized them—soon became the focus for reform. The key issue in the April 1900 city election was that of incorporating Santa Monica as a fifth-class city as a way to outlaw saloons. City trustees objected, noting that saloon licenses brought the town $2,500 a year. The leader of the local temperance movement, Frederick H. Rindge, owner of the Malibu Ranch, offered to give the town treasury an equal sum if the voters decided in favor of incorporation. When his group won a clear victory in the election, Rindge promptly dug out his checkbook and paid up.

The new ordinance, however, didn't exactly ban booze. It did allow restaurants to offer drinks along with meals that cost 25 cents or more; one store was licensed to sell alcoholic beverages in their original containers. Then, after some prominent citizens were convicted of violating the "meal" law, the trustees eliminated the minimum meal price requirement. Patrons could thus buy drinks as long as food accompanied the order. Such loosening of the nuts and bolts of the ordinance opened the door more than a crack. Soon "restaurants" were dispensing soda crackers with every shot—and some got by with handing patrons an empty cracker box.

Outraged reformers therefore pressed for a new law to ban outright all alcoholic beverages, but voters turned it down, 544 to 287. "Restaurant" and "bistro" licenses were issued without restriction from then on. Santa Monica remained a "wet" city until Prohibition began in 1920—and then quietly patronized speakeasies until its repeal in 1933.

Early in the century, before the film industry settled in Hollywood, moviemakers had popped up all over Southern California. Many of the earliest movie makers were refugees from New York who hoped to avoid paying patent fees to the Edison Company, which then controlled the rights to all motion picture technology. Others were trying to evade creditors, spouses, or the law.

By 1910 Santa Monica boasted three movie studios: Essanay, Vitagraph, and Kalem. In this era before sound, most of the studios' work was done on location, and the

The filming of an early silent movie on Santa Monica's beachfront attracted many curious spectators. Just like the beach, the Santa Monica Pier and its stunning carousel have been popular sites for many television and movie productions over the years. Courtesy, Elliott Welsh

42 SANTA MONICA

FACING PAGE, TOP: *Pascual Marquez opened his cliffside bathhouse on Santa Monica's beach in the 1880s. This photograph depicts the bathhouse, located just north of Chautauqua Boulevard, as it appeared in 1887. Courtesy, Elliott Welsh*

FACING PAGE, BOTTOM: *Sporting about 100 porcelain-lined tubs for salt and fresh water baths, a bowling alley, and a ballroom, the North Beach Bath House was Santa Monica's largest bathing facility from the time it opened in 1894 until it closed in the 1920s. The neighboring Arcadia Hotel is visible just a short distance down the beach. Courtesy, Santa Monica Public Library*

TOP, LEFT: *Youngsters enjoy the warm salt water offered by the North Beach Bath House Plunge circa 1900. The water in this huge pool, which ranged from 3 feet to 9 feet deep, was heated to 80 degrees and was refilled with fresh salt water daily. A dip cost 25 cents and visitors often watched bathers from the side bleachers. Courtesy, Elliott Welsh*

BOTTOM, LEFT: *The lavish Ocean Park Bath House resembled an Arabian palace with its colored domes and flagged towers. Built for $150,000 by A.R. Fraser, a partner with Abbot Kinney in the Ocean Park Improvement Co., this bathhouse was the pride of Ocean Park when it opened on the Fourth of July in 1905. Courtesy, Elliott Welsh*

ABOVE: Billed as the "Coney Island of the Pacific," the Million Dollar Pier was only one of a long line of amusement centers to delight Ocean Park visitors. Built by Alexander Fraser in 1910, this pier replaced the Horseshoe Pier, but burned down just two years after its construction. Courtesy, Dr. Robert Weinstein

RIGHT: Parents watch their children get whirled about on "The Whip," one of the many amusements enjoyed at the Looff Pleasure Pier in the early 1900s. Courtesy, Santa Monica Historical Society

brash young filmmakers thought nothing of setting up cameras in someone's backyard, on the beach, in the middle of a street, or in front of a store, usually unannounced, hardly ever with permission. Thus, when one of Santa Monica's most esteemed citizens opened her door to find Ben Turpin and Bronco Billy Anderson being filmed in a Wild West scene on her front lawn, she was told quite plainly to "get back in your house."

By 1915, however, all but one of the film studios had vanished—as quickly as they had arrived. The exception was Inceville, where "King of the Westerns" Thomas Ince filmed his silent masterpieces in Santa Ynez Canyon, above the Palisades. Ince moved his studio to Culver City in the 1920s.

Santa Monica's beachfront, increasingly popular, itself attracted many entrepreneurs. Michael Duffy put up the city's first bathhouse in 1877. Then, after the Los Angeles & Independence Railroad was built, Jones and Baker added the Santa Monica Bath House at the foot of the "99 Stairs," which provided access to the beach from the bluff of the palisades. Pascual Marquez built a cliffside bathhouse just north of Chautauqua Boulevard, and in 1887 the world-famous Arcadia Hotel, which included a bathhouse, went up on Ocean Avenue, between Colorado and Pico. The North Beach Bath House, a huge structure, 450 feet by 100 feet, with a huge freshwater pool, hot and cold saltwater baths, two dining rooms, a roof garden, bowling alley, ballroom, and elegant parlor, opened in 1894. With shops and the Pavilion Restaurant close by, this recreational venture became the focus of Santa Monica's beachfront fun zone. Ocean Park and Venice offered rival establishments.

The first Santa Monica Bay wharf was at Shoo Fly Landing, and other commercial wharves followed. The first pleasure pier went up in 1895, when real estate tycoon and visionary Abbot Kinney and his

popular with fishermen but failed to attract beachgoers. In 1904 he tried again in Venice, a few miles south; unfortunately the 1,700-foot structure was destroyed by winter storms just months after completion. Nevertheless, Kinney persisted; he shelled out $100,000 for a breakwater and rebuilt the Venice pier. At the time it was the only privately owned breakwater in the country.

Concessionaires and beachgoers then flocked to the area, attracting so much business away from Santa Monica piers that entrepreneurs stepped in. In 1905 George Merritt Jones and A.R. Fraser put up the Horseshoe Pier at the foot of Marine and Pier. The rival Crystal Pier was built at the foot of Hollister.

In 1910 Fraser and Jones replaced their enterprise with a larger one, the Million Dollar Pier, which boasted an amusement park. In 1912 the Million Dollar Pier went up in flames, which also destroyed much of neighboring Ocean Park. In its place arose three side-by-side piers, the Pickering, the G.M. Jones, and the Dome. In January 1924, though, these too were destroyed in a fire which also gutted the Dome and Rosemary theaters in Ocean Park.

Undaunted, a consortium that included film producer Sol Lesser, theater owner Adolph Ramish, and the Fox theater chain de-

partner, Francis Ryan, built a 500-foot structure in South Santa Monica.

Kinney had visions of a vast recreational complex that would draw visitors—and help sell the real estate he controlled in Ocean Park, which then included Venice. With the promise of a pier and amusement park that would attract riders, he induced the Santa Fe Railroad to extend track north from Ballona Lagoon in exchange for the land to build a depot; the line opened in June 1892.

Kinney's first pier was a disappointment. Several years later, around 1900, he replaced it with a 1,250-foot pier, which was

The Santa Monica Pier, with the Blue Streak Roller Coaster, the Bowling and Billiards Hall, and the famous La Monica Ballroom (far right), is shown in this 1923 view from Santa Monica Boulevard. At that time beach parking cost only 25 cents a day. Courtesy, Santa Monica Historical Society

ABOVE: The Ocean Skyway ride at Pacific Ocean Park took its passengers 75 feet above the Pacific Ocean for a six-minute, panoramic view of the Santa Monica Mountains, the bay, and the pier. The 28-acre park operated from 1958 to 1967. Courtesy, Santa Monica Historical Society

RIGHT: Lorings Lunch Room, on the Santa Monica Municipal Pier, boasted "No High Prices" in this 1925 photo, when hot dogs and soda pop cost a nickel each. Courtesy, Santa Monica Historical Society

veloped the James Lick and Ocean Park piers into amusement centers which operated with modest success for decades. In the early 1900s Charles Looff, a whimsical Dutchman who started at Coney Island in 1876 and then built amusement parks across the country, built Pleasure Pier at the foot of Colorado. An enormous complex of 178,200 square feet, it supported beneath its palm-leaf-festooned pagoda the 50-m.p.h. Blue Streak roller coaster, along with the Whip, Circle Swing, and What-Is-It rides. Looff wisely housed a fire station within the pagoda—as well as a picnic area. Nearby whirled the Hippodrome Carousel, a classic merry-go-round 50 feet in diameter, which sported 46 hand-carved wooden horses, as well as chariots, camels, goats, and giraffes. Picnickers were serenaded by the Royal Italian Band.

Looff sold his creation in 1917; in 1924 it was purchased by the Santa Monica Pleasure Pier Company, which extended the pier seaward and added the La Monica Ballroom, an Arabian Nights-inspired creation of spiraling towers and neon-framed minarets.

ABOVE: Beachgoers enjoy a typically delightful day along the Santa Monica shore in the mid-1920s. Note the style of swimwear worn by both men and women. The Santa Monica Pleasure Pier, with its roller coaster, and the La Monica Ballroom can be seen in the distance. Courtesy, Ed Tynan Photo Collection

LEFT: The Santa Monica Pier suffered severe storm damage from two fierce Pacific storms during the winter of 1983. Courtesy, Santa Monica Historical Society

Celebrated Residents

Over the years the Santa Monica Bay area has attracted many of the nation's most famous names. Among the many actors and entertainers who have lived in Santa Monica was stage and film star Leo Carrillo, whose family was among the city's earliest residents and whose ancestors include a city police chief and mayor. Media magnate William Randolph Hearst frequently stayed in the beachfront palace he built for his mistress, Marion Davies, the silent film star. Lovely, reclusive actress Greta Garbo found privacy here. Child star and later U.S. ambassador Shirley Temple was born in the city; such glamorous leading ladies as Joan Crawford, Barbara Stanwyck, Claudette Colbert, Loretta Young, Bette Davis, Carole Lombard, Kathryn Grayson, Norma Shearer, Mary Astor, Jean Arthur, Jeanette MacDonald and the beautiful Talmadge sisters, Norma, Natalie, and Constance, all made their homes in Santa Monica.

Academy Award winner Jane Fonda has long lived in the community. Santa Monica was also home for actress Betty Grable, every G.I.'s favorite World War II pinup, and "Funny Girl" vaudeville singer Fannie Brice lived in the community for many years. Ice skating star Sonja Henie performed all over the world but always came back to Santa Monica. Folk singer Joan Baez once lived in the Sea Castle Apartments near the Hippodrome Carousel. The singing Lennon sisters were born and raised in Venice, graduating from Santa Monica High School. They became famous on Lawrence Welk's TV show broadcast from Santa Monica's Aragon Ballroom.

Such leading men as Cary Grant, Clark Gable, Tyrone Power, William Powell, Fred MacMurray, Pat O'Brien, Don Ameche, Gilbert Roland, Robert Preston, Wendell Cory, Lionel Barrymore, Gary Cooper, Jeffrey Hunter, Peter Lawford, and Douglas Fairbanks, Jr., lived in Santa Monica while they made themselves legends of the silver screen.

Santa Monica has also had its share of funny folks, including Ha-

The sweet-faced silent screen star Mary Pickford, who lived on Santa Monica's Gold Coast with husband Douglas Fairbanks, Jr., is pictured here on her wedding day, March 28, 1920. Pickford won the Oscar for Coquette *in 1929, and continued to delight audiences in* Rebecca of Sunnybrook Farm *and many other films. Courtesy, The Hollywood Studio Museum*

Child star Shirley Temple, born in 1928 in Santa Monica, is pictured here signing war bonds to aid in the country's World War II efforts. Appearing in her first movie at age three, Temple was one of the highest-paid stars in Hollywood and probably the best-known child performer in the world. The star of Little Miss Marker *and* Heidi *retired from films in 1949 and in 1969 was appointed a U.S. delegate to the United Nations. In 1974 she became U.S. Ambassador to Ghana. Courtesy, Santa Monica Historical Society*

rold Lloyd, Harvey Korman, George Jessel, Stan Laurel, W.C. Fields, Dennis Day, Mickey Rooney, and the tragically slain Thelma Todd and her comic partner, Zasu Pitts.

Many motion picture executives, including Academy Award winning directors Mervyn LeRoy and Leo McCarey, producers David O. Selznick and Irving Thalberg, and studio moguls Louis B. Mayer (MGM), Joseph Schenck (United Artists, Twentieth Century Fox), Hal Roach and Harry Warner (Warner Brothers), and Darryl Zanuck (Twentieth Century Fox), have owned grand homes in Santa Monica. Continuing the tradition is TV writer/producer Steven Bochco.

Former President Ronald Reagan lived in Pacific Palisades, not far from astrologer and author Sydney Omarr. One of the richest men in the world, oil billionaire J. Paul Getty, built a Roman villa just north of the city to house his art collection. Aviation pioneers who called Santa Monica home include Waldo Waterman; Donald W. Douglas, founder of the Douglas Aircraft Company; innovative designer William P. Lear; and General Jimmy Doolittle, a racing champion who led the bombing raid on Tokyo in the darkest days of World War II.

In the era between world wars, Santa Monica Canyon and adjacent Pacific Palisades became home to some of the world's most gifted writers, who were attracted by the area's solitude and natural beauty. Among them was Will Rogers, who bought land in Rustic Canyon, topographically the northern end of Santa Monica Canyon. Rogers, who wrote a newspaper column and became world renowned for his down-to-earth humor and wry wisdom, was an avid polo player and kept horses on his property.

Other noted residents included novelist and social satirist Christopher Isherwood and composer Ferde Grofe, who wrote *Grand Canyon Suite*, his best-known work, and many other symphonies in his home on Adelaide Drive, above the canyon.

A great influx of European writers to the area began in the 1930s. Aldous Huxley, Thomas and Heinrich Mann, Alfred Doeblin, Stefan Zweig, Ludwig Marcuse, playwright Bertolt Brecht, and many others took up extended residence in novelist Lion Feuchtwanger's Villa Aurora, a 22-room, Spanish Provincial mansion.

This structure was built by the *Los Angeles Times* in 1928 as a demonstration of the ultimate in residential technology. Feuchtwanger, a Jewish refugee from Hitler's Germany, bought the house in 1941. With a library of 36,000 rare and valuable books, including thousands of first editions dating back to the fifteenth century, it became a center

Humorist Will Rogers, an ardent fan of flying and a friend to many aviators, was photographed with Charles Lindbergh, the first pilot to fly solo nonstop across the Atlantic Ocean. Rogers died in a 1935 plane crash with his friend, aviator Wiley Post. Courtesy, Santa Monica Historical Society

for refugee German writers and their friends. When Feuchtwanger died in 1958, his wife, Marta, continued as the doyenne of the German intellectual community in Southern California. After her death in 1987, the library and house were left to the University of Southern California.

Humorist Irvin S. Cobb, meanwhile, penned his sidesplitting syndicated columns from Santa Monica. Screenwriter Anita Loos wrote *Some Like It Hot* and other cinematic treasures when she resided here.

Playwrights Bertolt Brecht and Rachel Crothers also penned some of their best works while living in the city. Muralist and writer Hugo Ballin left his largest works on the walls of City Hall. Master painters Sam Francis and Richard Diebenkorn moved to the city for its fantastic light.

Cosmetics manufacturer Merle Norman, razor blade tycoon King Gillette, and automobile stoplight inventor Robert E. Olsen all set up shop in Santa Monica, where they lived. Former U.S. Senator John Tunney resides in the same city that Jack Dempsey—whom his father, Gene, defeated to become heavyweight champion of the world—also called home. Eugene F. Bizcailuz, the legendary lawman, lived in Santa Monica while he was Los Angeles County sheriff from 1932 to 1958.

Santa Monica has been the home of many tennis champions, including Marion Jones, daughter of the city founder; May Sutton Bundy; Elizabeth "Bunny" Ryan, and Gertrude "Gorgeous Gussie" Moran. National race car champion Phil Hill is a Santa Monica native.

Orchestra leaders Horace Heidt and Red Norvo lived in the community for decades, as did Nobel laureate poet Maurice Maeterlinck, famed meterologist Dr. Jacob Bjerkness, and nutrition scientist Nathan Pritikin.

The stunning Marion Davies beachfront estate in Santa Monica, which included tennis courts, dog kennels, and three guest houses, was perhaps the largest and most luxurious seaside home built on the Pacific coastline in the early 1900s. Courtesy, Dr. Robert Weinstein

Upward of 50,000 spectators turned out for La Monica's opening night, creating Santa Monica's first traffic jam. The dance floor swayed 'neath the feet of 5,000 tripping the Light Fantastic and other popular terpsichorean feats of the era; an equal number of wallflowers looked on from the sidelines. For decades after, the ballroom was jammed on weekend and summer nights. People from all over the world came to listen and dance to the music of bandleaders Abe Lyman and Paul Whiteman.

Sharing worldwide fame with the La Monica was the Aragon Ballroom on adjacent Lick Pier, which also featured the leading orchestras of its day. While the Depression severely cramped the styles of both ballrooms, World War II brought a huge influx of aircraft industry workers and military men into the area. Thus for much of the war the La Monica served as a bivouac for some 5,000 troops responsible for protecting the coastline. At the time, strict blackout precautions precluded most nighttime activities, including dancing, although other pier concessions continued to operate during daylight.

Then, after the war, the ballrooms began to swing to a different beat. In the early 1950s, Spade Cooley, a fiddler and crooner in the country and western manner, originated his weekly TV shows from the La Monica. He soon moved to the Aragon, but after he was convicted of murdering his wife, Cooley was forced to limit his performances to captive audiences.

The Aragon, for its part, became a coast-to-coast household word in the 1950s when Lawrence Welk and his Champagne Orchestra began weekly TV broadcasts from its ballroom. Next, in 1961, the Aragon was converted to a skating rink, but never did well. The structure was torn down two years later, in 1963.

Meanwhile, in 1958, CBS Broadcasting and the Hollywood Turf Club had put up $15 million to transform Ocean Park Pier into Pacific Ocean Park, known as POP. Designed to compete with Disneyland, POP drew two million visitors its first year, yet it was never able to generate the unique brand of storybook excitement that Disney cartoon characters provided. POP thus went into bankruptcy in 1967; it became a moldering eyesore until it was finally torn down in 1974, after lengthy litigation.

Santa Monica Pier, next to the Pleasure Pier, was built in 1920 with the proceeds of a $75,000 bond issue. After construction of a breakwater a lower deck was added, in 1935. For decades this pier served as a backdrop for innumerable motion pictures and TV series as well as commercials. It stood in for the Venice Pier for *Inside Daisy Clover*, starring the young Natalie Wood.

In 1942 Walter and Enid Newcomb acquired the pier from Ernest Pickering, who had bought it from the Pleasure Pier organization. After decades of exposure to the elements, in the 1960s the structure began to deteriorate. In 1967 the city attempted to redevelop the pier and its environs, but voters turned down the bond issue. Then in 1973 the city council bought the pier from the Newcombs and ordered its demolition. Appalled citizen groups placed an initiative on the city ballot; Proposition One, the Pier Preservation Ordinance, was approved by voters. In the winter of 1983, however, two huge Pacific storms battered the coast, causing extensive damage to the pier.

Unquestionably Santa Monica Bay's best-known historic landmark and community resource, the pier was named a Santa Monica City Landmark in 1976. Renovation began in April 1987, so the landmark pier can once again serve as the centerpiece of Santa Monica's bayfront recreation zone, a tangible link with the city's colorful past.

Locations

Santa Monica Pier is located at the foot of Colorado Avenue. This historic landmark continues to attract thousands of visitors daily.

Carousel Building, on the Looff/Newcomb Pleasure Pier, was designated a National Historic Landmark in 1988. The carousel and its surroundings were transformed into Chicago, circa 1920, as a setting for *The Sting*, the Oscar-winning film starring Paul Newman and Robert Redford.

Sand and Sea Club, the former Marion Davies estate, was built by her paramour, William Randolph Hearst, at 415 Palisades Beach Road. The architect of one of the buildings, the Marion Davies Guest House—now a City Landmark—was Julia Morgan, who also designed Hearst's San Simeon castle. The main house, once the largest, most luxurious beach house on the Pacific Coast, included tennis courts, dog kennels, three guest houses, and two swimming pools. It was demolished in 1957.

Sunset Memorial Seat is found in Palisades Park. This spot, where John P. Jones often came to watch the sunset, is graced with a bench donated in 1923 by his son-in-law, Robert David Farquhar.

Will Rogers Monument, erected in 1952, commemorates humorist Will Rogers' many contributions to our nation's storehouse of wit. The monument stands at the intersection of Ocean Avenue and Santa Monica Boulevard, the terminus of the Will Rogers Highway, known as the "Main Street of America."

Wilshire Palisades Building, the site of the former home of Arcadia Bandini de Baker, is located at 1229 Ocean Avenue. The original building was demolished in 1936.

The Queen Anne-style **Gussie Moran House,** built circa 1895, is found at 1323 Ocean Avenue. Moran, who scandalized staid Wimbledon audiences with her modish, scanty costumes, lived there for many years.

CHAPTER FOUR

More Than the Sum of Its Parts

Students of the Sixth Street School pose for their annual class picture in the early 1920s. Courtesy, Santa Monica Historical Society

INCORPORATION

As Santa Monica grew from the land developers' vision into a thriving, vibrant city, so were born the institutions that underpin a community: government agencies, churches, libraries, medical facilities, clubs, leagues, societies, and associations.

In 1880 Santa Monica and Ballona Township had only 417 year-round residents. Thus when some of these talked of incorporating as a city, others feared that a government would be prohibitively expensive when borne by such a small number of taxpayers. Arguing for cityhood were merchants who believed incorporation would permit legal business licenses that would discourage competition from more established companies out of Los Angeles.

Few were more anxious about this rivalry than William S. Vawter, proprietor of the city's first general store and a prominent real estate developer. He sought an exclusive franchise to build a streetcar system; a Los Angeles consortium was also after

53

ABOVE: Around the time of Santa Monica's incorporation and early commercial development, trespassers known as "squatters" lived in these beachfront makeshift huts until forced to leave by the official landowners. This 1887 view also shows the famous "99 Steps," which led from the palisades bluffs to the ocean. Courtesy, Ed Tynan Photo Collection

RIGHT: Santa Monica pioneer William S. Vawter, a prominent real estate developer, established the towns first general store, lumber yard, and planing mill. In 1886, he built the first horse-drawn streetcar line, which ran between Santa Monica and the Sawtelle Soldiers Home. Courtesy, Santa Monica Historical Society

the franchise. After real estate, the leading Santa Monica industry was bathhouses; owners of the larger establishments, including J.W. Scott, builder of the Arcadia Hotel, felt that after incorporation hefty license fees would discourage competition from newcomers.

A ballot for incorporation was held in April 1886—and after numerous recounts, lost by one vote. In November 1886 a second election was held; 97 voted for and 71 against cityhood. Thus, after approval by the California legislature, Santa Monica became a sixth-class city in 1887. The board of trustees, effectively the city council, was elected on the same ballot: John Steere, Dr. E.C. Folsom, A.E. Ladd, William S. Vawter, and J.W. Scott. The board chose Steere to serve as temporary chairman, in effect the city's first mayor, with Vawter as acting secretary. E.K. Chapin was appointed town treasurer; F.C. McKinne, town clerk.

Soon after incorporation Vawter got his franchise; horse-drawn streetcar service on Ocean Avenue began in June 1887. Bathhouse license fees were established, though the council, despite Scott's machinations, wisely set them low enough to encourage

competition, which ultimately helped the city to flourish.

Having been duly elected, meanwhile, the new government set about passing laws. Its first ordinance, on January 17, 1887, provided punishments for keepers of "dis-

In 1890, two employees of H. Hergetts Company meat market proudly pose outside of their establishment, which was located on Third Street in the heart of Santa Monica's business district. The sidewalk in front of this store had just been paved by the new city government. Courtesy, Elliott Welsh

orderly houses" and for those convicted of "disorderly" conduct. The same day, the government created a two-dollar "street poll tax" for every adult male between the ages of 21 and 60; the money would go to build streets. A third ordinance, passed two weeks later, prohibited houses of prostitution and "ill fame." A law against vagrancy was put into effect soon afterward: anyone capable of work but refusing to look for it and anyone caught begging "as a business," as well as those "associates" of "known thieves" or anyone who slept in barns, outhouses, vessels, sheds, or shops or who was "a common drunkard" or a prostitute, was to be given the choice of 90 days in the "grey bar hotel" or a $90 fine. A singular exemption was provided—for native Americans.

Once these laws were enacted it became obvious that the new town needed a jail. In March 1887 the trustees voted $600 for a combination jail and animal pound. Because they needed land on which to build, they awarded council chairman Steere $50 a year to rent a 30-foot-by-50-foot portion of a lot he owned. No one bid on the new complex, however, and the trustees rescinded Steere's lease and gave one instead to W.O. Baxter.

Such shenanigans did not go unnoticed by the electorate. In the 1888 election, Steere, Ladd, and Scott were dumped,

Ed Tynan, who immigrated from Ireland in 1879, was Santa Monica's first official postman. Tynan is pictured here in 1890, while delivering the mail in his horse and buggy. Courtesy, Ed Tynan Photo Collection

while Vawter and Dr. Folsom were retained. Thomas Rhodes, Thomas A. Lewis, and former Los Angeles city marshal Juan J. Carrillo were elected to the new board. Carrillo, whose son, Leo, would become a world-famous actor, was elected chairman and honorary mayor in 1890. He served until 1897.

So functioned the board of trustee structure until Prohibitionist reformers reshaped the power balance. A board of freeholders was then elected in 1905 to prepare a city charter. On March 28, 1906, when voters approved the document, Santa Monica became a charter city.

The new city government provided for seven council members, elected from their respective wards, and a mayor. The council members, however, were part-time politicians, who continued to devote much of their time to their own businesses. By 1914 it was apparent that important city matters were too often delayed. A second charter was thus drawn, providing for the election of three full-time commissioners. In 1915 Maxwell K. Barretto, a former town marshal, was elected commissioner of finance; William H. Carter became commissioner of

The People's Republic

For many decades, Santa Monica was, as *Newsweek* once put it, "the pot of gold at the end of Wilshire Boulevard," an affluent, largely conservative community dominated by business interests. From the late 1940s through the 1970s, however, vigorous real estate development sowed the seeds of its own undoing.

As more and more apartment buildings went up, so too did the city's renter population. At the same time, real estate values skyrocketed, partly because of soaring nationwide inflation. Gentrification in rundown neighborhoods brought an influx of young, upwardly mobile home owners and a wave of apartment-to-condominium conversions. As soaring real estate values triggered rapid rent rises, the city's middle-class renters, representing about 80 percent of its voters, were squeezed. A 1978 rent control initiative was voted down.

This caught the attention of Ocean Park resident Tom Hayden, a noted sixties radical who headed a statewide organization, the Campaign for Economic Democracy (CED). Hayden saw in rent control a grassroots issue that had broad political support among those he considered his natural constituency. Mobilizing the elderly, as well as liberals, neighborhood groups, and renters, he formed a coalition, Santa Monicans for Renters Rights (SMRR).

In 1979, when Santa Monica landlords failed to stabilize rents in the wake of Proposition 13, which drastically cut property taxes, SMRR pushed through a tough city rent control ordinance and captured a pair of city council seats. Soon SMRR candidates won control of the new rent control board, and in April 1981 the coalition won four city council seats to control the council. They named feisty Ruth Yannatta Goldway, 36, as mayor, and put her husband, urban planner Derek Shearer, on the planning commission. A bureaucracy was created to deal with complaints and challenges to the statute.

With a goal of ending what they termed the "Manhattanization of Santa Monica," the new city council stopped 82 construction projects and allowed 51 others to continue only after forcing developers to add low- and middle-income housing, child care centers and job programs in lieu of steep "arts and social service" fees.

Developers, home owners, and landlords responded with outraged cries of extortion. They distributed thousands of hammer-and-sickle bumper stickers bearing the legend "Welcome to the People's Republic of Santa Monica" and warned that the rent control coalition was undermining the city's economic base. Some incensed landlords began to withhold their apartments from the market—up to 2,500 units—and announced they would rent only to "felons and foreigners" who could not vote.

Rent control thus polarized Santa Monica politics. Tom Hayden, for one, used the issue to propel himself into a state assembly seat.

And rent control remains a controversial issue. Landlord and home-owner groups have repeatedly attempted to repeal the statute through the initiative process, while renters' groups have agitated for modifications giving renters greater rights, such as the privilege of subletting their apartments.

public works; and Samuel L. Berkeley became commissioner of public safety and mayor. He later appointed himself police chief.

This arrangement lasted until the city was rechartered in 1946. The present system calls for the election of seven at-large council members. The council appoints a city manager and city attorney. Except for the personal staffs of these two officials, all other city workers are employed through civil service.

Until a nationwide executive search turned up Randall M. Dorton, who was appointed in 1947, the city engineer, Maurice King, was named acting city manager. Dorton was the dean of California's city managers. His track record extended back to 1919, when he almost single-handedly cleaned up a den of corruption while running the city of Pittsburg, in Northern California. As a career civil servant with a widely recognized talent for organization and supervision, under his tutelage the city's finances were strengthened while property tax rates declined, and city services were vastly improved and broadened. Among his accomplishments were construction of the Civic Auditorium, a new civic center, police headquarters, and two branch libraries. He was also largely responsible for improvements in the water system, as well as the creation of parks and recreation projects and the redevelopment of Ocean Park. Dorton retired in 1959.

He was succeeded by his right-hand man, George Bundy, patriarch of one of the community's oldest families. Bundy served less than three years; a series of heart attacks precipitated his retirement. Nevertheless, for many years afterward he continued to be active in public affairs.

POLICE DEPARTMENT

Santa Monica's first elected town marshal was Hamilton Baggs, Jr., but after he refused to accept a $900 annual salary, the board of trustees appointed Michael Moon in his place. Although a night watchman was appointed in 1888—merchants paid two-thirds of his $60 per month salary—the city did not have a full-time policeman until 1898.

In 1888 Marshal Moon was replaced by A.J. Smith, who resigned a few months into his term and was replaced by George Kibben, who also resigned within months. Maxwell Barretto, then constable of the town-

In 1897, Max Barretto left his position at Port Los Angeles to become Santa Monica's first chief of police. Courtesy, Santa Monica Historical Society

In 1909, the Santa Monica Police Department posed with Juan Carrillo (center), the city's first police court judge. One of Carrillo's 13 children, Leo, was destined to become a star of the stage and screen. Courtesy, Santa Monica Historical Society

ship court, became the new marshal. Meanwhile, Juan Carrillo's son, Alfredo, became night watchman. Together Barretto and Carrillo comprised the city's entire law enforcement squad. Carrillo was later succeeded by Deputy "Dad" Brighton, who was famous for vanquishing the notorious Evans-Sontag stage robber gang.

For much of these early years the police devoted the majority of their time to collaring drunks, chiefly those staggering out of the saloons lining Broadway (then called Utah). Lacking a paddy wagon, the usual method of transport to the lockup was a wheelbarrow.

Barretto, meanwhile, was elected marshal every two years, until his resignation in 1894 to become Port Los Angeles deputy customs inspector. In 1897 he returned to Santa Monica office; in the interval the trustees had created a five-man police department and changed the title of its boss to chief of police. The chief's duties included tax and license fee collection, at least until 1908, when the office of tax collector was established and the police department enlarged. The new department provided for nine patrolmen, but because of budgetary considerations only six could be on the payroll at a time.

In 1909 Juan Carrillo was appointed police court judge. When Barretto was elected city treasurer in 1911, the chief of police was Ellis Randall, a former police sergeant. Randall modernized the department, adding a detective bureau, two motorcycle officers, and a call box system.

FIRE DEPARTMENT

The Santa Monica Hose and Hook and Ladder Company, organized in March 1889, boasted 46 volunteers, including the

The Santa Monica fire station, located at Fourth Street and Oregon Avenue (Santa Monica Boulevard) behind City Hall, is shown in this 1910 photograph. The horse-drawn hose cart was later replaced by motorized fire equipment in 1913. Courtesy, Santa Monica Historical Society

Puritas was a major bottled water distributor in Santa Monica in the early 1900s. Courtesy, Santa Monica Historical Society

town's most prominent citizens. Robert Eckert, a pioneer member of the Los Angeles Fire Department, was chosen foreman and president. Equipment included 2,000 feet of hose, two hose carts, and a hook-and-ladder truck. In 1900 the city council appropriated funds for a combination hose wagon and chemical engine, as well as a team of horses. Firemen served without pay; benefit balls and other events were staged in order to create a relief fund for those injured in the line of duty.

WATER SUPPLY

Water has always been in short supply in Santa Monica. During the summer drought of 1912, water was so scarce that when a fire started near Venice Pier, all firemen could do was let it burn itself out—and it destroyed about three-fourths of the southern end of Santa Monica. At first the city was supplied by artesian-fed springs near what is now University High. Later a pump was installed on Venice Pier to provide sea water for fire hydrants. In 1916 the city floated a $667,000 bond issue to purchase four privately owned water companies (City Water Company, Ocean Park Water Company, Santa Monica Water Company, and Irwin Heights Water Company).

Nevertheless, more water was needed during rapid city growth in the 1920s. In 1923 another bond issue was approved, and Charnock Wells in Mar Vista became the city's principal supplier. Yet even this wasn't enough.

Los Angeles, meanwhile, had plenty of water, thanks to the aqueduct supplying the city from the Owens Valley. Voters in Sawtelle, Venice, and Palms would eventually choose annexation by Los Angeles in order to get a share of that water; Santa Monicans, however, remained opposed to annexation. The Bay City thus continued to drill wells, until the creation of the Metropolitan Water District (MWD) in 1928 allowed municipalities to purchase state project water, chiefly from Northern California, at reasonable rates. Today about 37 percent of the city's water comes from wells; the balance, from the MWD.

MEDICAL SERVICES

While no community is complete without facilities for medical care, Santa Monica has long been blessed with some of the finest healers and physicians in the West. The local Indians relied on shamans; the first Western medical care arrived in the leather bags carried by Franciscan missionaries. With these crude instruments the padres were able to perform a few basic surgical proce-

Santa Monica Hospital was established in 1926 by physicians William Mortensen and August Hromadka, and was run in the manner of a hotel. The 60-bed hospital, pictured here circa 1926, eventually became part of the Santa Monica Medical Center. Courtesy, Santa Monica Historical Society

dures. In 1805 and 1825, for example, Franciscans were reported to have performed cesarean sections on women whose lives were at risk in childbirth. Otherwise the priests and the handful of Spanish physicians who settled here during the Mexican period depended upon herbs and other homeopathic remedies, including several borrowed from native American culture.

The first Anglo physician to practice in Santa Monica was Dr. E.C. Folsom, who, as previously described, became a member of the first city council and also served as the health officer. Doctors Chaffey and Rogers followed, taking out ads in the *Outlook* in which they offered "specialized electrical and compound oxygen treatments."

Another early physician was Dr. N.H. Hamilton, who arrived in 1893 and shared offices in the Clarendon Hotel, at what is now Broadway and Third, with Doctors Lynn Case, Smith, H.L. Coffman, and Urquhart. Whatever their complaint, in addition to any other therapies performed, Hamilton's patients were all instructed to drink nothing but Puritas Water, a popular brand of bottled water. Furthermore, he "toned" their bodies by administering mild shocks of static electricity. And because he felt his office assistants did not properly appreciate each patient's financial status or emotional makeup, Hamilton insisted on preparing each patient's bill personally, submitting it at what he felt was the most propitious psychological moment.

In 1906 Dr. William Mortensen, a 27-year-old emigré from Wisconsin, decided that Santa Monica, with seven doctors, was too risky for a new practice and opted for Palms—until he returned to Santa Monica five years later. He saw most of his patients on house calls, for which he charged two dollars; office calls were $1.00 to $1.25. His patients included victims of one of Santa Monica's earliest auto accidents, a man with three gunshot wounds, several people who had teeth extracted, and many childbirths. Although he prospered financially, nearly a fourth of his fees were uncollectible. Mortensen's wife, Florence, was also an M.D., though he refused to allow her to practice.

In 1907 Dr. August Hromadka, a Nebraskan, gave up his practice in Mexicali and established an office near his new home at Sawtelle and Santa Monica boulevards. On his first day at this location he treated 13 members of the pioneer Marquez family for botulism poisoning.

For years Hromadka's office had the only telephone in what was then largely a farming community; he encouraged his neighbors to use it, attracting a steady stream of visitors at all hours of the day and night. Known as a kindly man, he often bought and personally delivered medicine for his poorest patients.

Hromadka bicycled to local house calls, accompanied by his toddler son, John, secure in an affixed basket. Visiting patients farther away in Topanga Canyon by horse and buggy, he once narrowly escaped injury in a cattle stampede. Later he bought one of the community's first automobiles. However, it frequently broke down and had to be towed ignominiously behind a team of horses. While making house calls at night in Santa Monica Canyon, he routinely admonished John (his companion still) to remain in the car—to avoid possible attack from wolves—while he went inside and treated the patient.

Santa Monica's first hospital was established in 1908 at Fourth and Pacific in Ocean Park. The Santa Monica Hospital, a joint venture by several physicians, led by Dr. M.L. Loomis, was a financial failure and closed in 1910. It was reopened, however, in 1911 by three graduate nurses from Chicago, the Lowry sisters, and was renamed St. Catherine's. It had but 30 beds.

Meanwhile, Hromadka and Mortensen, close friends and colleagues who frequently assisted and consulted each other, went to Vienna several times for surgical training between 1910 and 1913. Afterward Hromadka began to specialize in urology. Mortensen opened a second office in Santa Monica in 1911. A few years later, returning late from a house call, he was shot in the leg by a bandit who stole his medical bag. Fortunately the wound was not serious.

Until 1926 Mortensen and Hromadka did most of their hospital work at the Loamshire, established in 1913 on Princeton. But, as Santa Monica grew, both physicians saw the need for a larger and more modern hospital; the nearest such facility was in Hollywood. They thus secured property at 16th and Arizona and tried to drum up financial support from other community physicians, as well as from the city council. However, no one was willing to invest in what was considered a high-risk proposition. Mortgaging their own homes, Mortensen and Hromadka then borrowed $50,000 from Aubrey Austin, Sr., the man who would in 1933 purchase controlling interest in Santa Monica Savings Bank, now known as Santa Monica Bank. Nevertheless, $50,000 wasn't enough; Austin thus made them an unsecured personal loan for the rest.

The brick, three-story, 60-bed hospital opened on July 26, 1926. The first patient, a woman in labor, was admitted during the open house festivities.

Santa Monica Hospital was built in the style of a hotel. Room rates were four dollars a day for wards, five dollars for semi-private rooms, and six dollars for private rooms. Private corner rooms were slightly more expensive.

In 1942, after Hromadka's death, the hospital was turned over to the Lutheran Hospital Society. Today Santa Monica Medical Center is one of the city's greatest assets, serving the entire community and drawing many of the region's most esteemed physicians. Its nine-story tower on 16th Street was completed in 1971. In October 1986 the Merle Norman Pavilion, a six-story patient care facility, opened. The project was funded in part by Merle Norman Cosmetics, which began in Santa Monica.

In 1920 the Archbishop of Los Angeles, John J. Cantwell, became convinced that a Catholic hospital was needed in the Santa Monica area. After many years he succeeded in gathering support for this project among lay Catholics and the Sisters of Charity of Leavenworth, a Kansas-based nursing order, to establish a facility in Santa Monica. By 1939 the necessary money had been raised, and construction began on 22nd Street. In 1942 an 87-bed hospital, named for St. John the Apostle, opened its doors.

Today St. John's Hospital and Health Center handles 551 inpatients and thousands more outpatients through a complex of clinics and community outreach services. It is sometimes known as the "Hospital to the Stars" because of the constant stream of Hollywood luminaries who have been treated there.

SCHOOLS

Santa Monica's first school was established in March 1876 in the First Presbyterian Church. The town paid the church $25 a month rent, and employed H.P. McKusick as teacher with a salary of $100 a month, a re-

Children from surrounding farms and ranches attended the one-room Canyon School in Santa Monica Canyon, shown here in 1894, the same year the building became a public school. Now the library of Canyon Elementary School, this building is the oldest school structure in Los Angeles that is still in use today. Courtesy, Santa Monica Historical Society

spectable figure for that era. The first day 52 students were enrolled in 11 classes of three grades. By April a total of 77 students were enrolled. By the end of that first school year, enrollment was more than 120, though average attendance was less than 70. A second teacher, Alice Whitton, was hired to teach primary grades.

Only after voting to establish the school did the council find a way to pay for it: by passing a tax of 60 cents per $100 in assessed property value. Senator John P. Jones and Colonel Robert S. Baker donated two adjacent lots on Sixth, between Arizona and Oregon (now Santa Monica Boulevard), for construction of a two-story school building; the Sixth Street School, as it was called, was completed in the summer of 1876. With such equipment and supplies as blackboards, desks, an outdoor privy, and stationery, the school cost more than $4,200, or virtually all that had been collected in taxes.

Finding and keeping teachers and administrators in the early years was a challenge. To fulfill the need for a strong disciplinarian, J.H.P. Williams was elected principal in 1881. Late on a December evening that year he appeared at the rehearsal for a school play being held in the vacant Santa

Monica Hotel. The hotel caretaker, upset that the principal had arrived so late, began to chastise him. Williams whipped out a revolver and shot the man. At his trial for attempted murder, Williams was acquitted after testifying that he mistook a pipe protruding from the caretaker's pocket for a pistol. The Board of Trustees nevertheless decided to fire him.

For many years Santa Monica's school board encouraged corporal punishment to discipline rambunctious pupils. One of the more infamous practitioners of this art was Principal E.P. Howell, who devised a "torture instrument" of two leather belts fastened with copper rivets, which he applied liberally behind the knees of his young victims. Despite complaints from parents, the school board ruled in 1891 that teachers were authorized to whip students and that any student who refused "just punishment" would be immediately suspended.

In 1893, however, after still more parental complaints, the board forbade teachers from whipping students. Outraged teachers submitted a petition protesting this change. Not until threatened with the loss of their jobs did they back down. Teachers and principals continued to spank and slap pupils for many years, however. Not until 1906 did the city charter contain a restriction against hitting students, "except in the presence of or with the written consent of the parent or guardian of the pupil."

As Santa Monica continued to grow as a residential community, the schools grew with it. An additional school was built in 1890 for "South Santa Monica," later to become Ocean Park; the Washington School would eventually be rebuilt and today is the site of the Santa Monica Alternative School. In 1891 high school courses were added to the Sixth Street School, under a law passed by the state legislature establishing high schools. In 1894 a one-room school was added in Santa Monica Canyon to serve its burgeoning population. In 1895, $15,000 was voted for a Lincoln High School at 10th Street and Arizona Avenue, the site of today's Olympic High School, a continuation school.

The construction of Lincoln High School in 1897 started a school-building boom which would bring eight schools in 18 years. Among them was the Garfield School at Seventh and Michigan Avenue,

A teacher and her students take advantage of the cool ocean breezes off Santa Monica Bay in an effort to beat the heat in this outdoor classroom circa 1940. Courtesy, Santa Monica Historical Society

The early Methodist Episcopal Church, pictured here in the foreground about 1882, was founded on October 15, 1875, when it had a minister but no permanent place of worship. In the background is the First Presbyterian Church, also established in 1875, when it had a congregation but no minister. Courtesy, Santa Monica Historical Society

where Santa Monica's first PTA was established in 1910. A new Garfield School was built in 1933 at 16th and Colorado. In 1907 Jefferson School was built on the site of the city's first school, which was torn down.

By 1910 a new high school was needed to replace Lincoln High. Ocean Park residents were clamoring for a high school in their area, while Santa Monica residents wanted the school located to the north. As a compromise the board of education chose 13 acres between the two communities on the 120-foot-high Prospect Hill, then an open lot which overlooked the ocean. With $200,000 approved by voters, Santa Monica High School was built on its present site, its cornerstone laid April 11, 1912.

In 1929 Santa Monica Junior College was established and assigned quarters on the second floor of Santa Monica High School, with an initial enrollment of 153 students. Soon afterward the college outgrew its quarters and moved across the street to the old Garfield School building. When that structure was declared unsafe in the wake of the 1933 Long Beach earthquake, classes moved into a group of wood-frame tents affectionately known as "Splinterville."

The 1933 earthquake severely damaged Santa Monica's schools; most were torn down, and tents were immediately set up so students could return to classes. An estimated 1,400 men worked to make the schools earthquake-safe, backed by federal grants and local bonds—expenditures reached $3 million upon completion.

The schools were open again by 1937 and the school district was ready to expand, as student population increased by 40 percent between 1938 and 1948. Many schools were added after World War II, including Will Rogers School at 14th and Maple in 1949. Several were in Malibu, to save children there a long bus ride to Santa Monica.

In 1937 Santa Monica Technical School

was founded at 22nd and Pico; in 1938 an evening school was established to offer trade extension courses. In 1945 all three schools were consolidated into a single institution, Santa Monica College. In 1948 ground was broken for a new, 44-acre campus at 1900 Pico Boulevard, and in 1969 vocational activities were transferred to this location. A satellite campus was opened at Malibu Park Junior High School in 1975, and the Humanities Center at the Santa Monica Airport opened in 1988. Offering transfer and vocational classes and granting the Associate in Arts Degree, Santa Monica College now accommodates some 20,000 students.

CHURCHES

The First Presbyterian Church in Santa Monica was established by the Reverend Dr. A.F. White in September 1875. Of its 12 charter members, eight were women, half of whom were members of the Vawter family. On January 20, 1876, two congregants, Mattie Mountain and Alfred Hayes, were joined together as man and wife in the new church. Because no Presbyterian minister was available, the Reverend John Crum, a Methodist, officiated over Santa Monica's first marriage.

Santa Monica's Methodist Episcopal Church was founded on October 15, 1875, the Reverend Crum presiding. Thus began a debate, still unsettled, over which was the first church, the Presbyterians, who had a congregation but no minister, or the Methodists, who had a minister but no place of their own in which to worship. The issue is likely to go unsettled; however, the two congregations remain bound by the warm ties forged at their inceptions.

The community's earliest non-Indian settlers, of course, were devout Catholics, and on July 28, 1877, the first Mass was celebrated in Santa Monica. Seven years later St. Monica's Church was organized at Third and Santa Monica. Leading St. Monica's parish in 1886 was the dynamic Father Patrick Hawe, who went on to conduct the first Catholic service in Ocean Park in 1902, opening the way for the organization of St. Clement's Church in 1904. Father Hawe also established Trinity Mission at the Sawtelle Soldiers Home in 1903, and St. Anne's Church at 2017 Colorado in 1908. St. Monica's moved to its present location at California and Seventh in 1925, when its cathedral-like church was completed.

Meanwhile, the Sisters of the Holy Names established the Academy of Holy Names at Third and Arizona, which was dedicated February 22, 1901. Regular services for St. Augustine by-the-Sea Episcopal Church began as early as 1876, and a redwood church was constructed in 1888 at 1227 Fourth Street, where it stood until 1966, when it was destroyed by fire. The church was rebuilt in 1969, continuing its distinction as the oldest church in the city still in its original location.

A group of Baptists founded the South Santa Monica Sunday School in 1890, and a Baptist chapel was built two years later. The Trinity Baptist Church was formed in 1914, and its church built at Caliifornia and 10th in 1926; the church was rebuilt on this site in 1950.

The First Church of Christ, Scientist, organized in Santa Monica in 1897, and built the first Christian Science church on the West Coast in 1900. A new church was built on the site at Arizona and Fifth in 1963.

Between 1900 and 1925 three major black congregations were formed. The first was Colored Methodist Episcopal, now known as the Christian Methodist Episcopal Church, based since 1908 at the Phillips Chapel at Fourth and Bay streets. Calvary Baptist Church was founded in 1920, and First African Methodist Episcopal Church was formed in 1923.

Other churches established by the early 1930s were Pilgrim Lutheran Church, Santa Monica Free Methodist Church, the Seventh Day Adventist Church, Church of the

City of Santa Monica Designated Landmarks

Name & Address	Date Designated	Date of Construction; Architect/Builder
Rapp Saloon 1438 Second St.	Aug. 20, 1975	1875; Spencer & Pugh, Bricklayers
Miles Playhouse 1130 Lincoln Blvd.	Oct. 15, 1975	1929; John Byers
Santa Monica Pier Foot of Colorado Ave.	Aug. 17, 1976	1916 (Looff Pier); Various builders
Miramar Moreton Bay Fig Tree Ocean Ave. at Wilshire Blvd.	Aug. 17, 1976	Planted circa 1880
Methodist Episcopal Church 2621 Second St.	Jan. 4, 1977	1875-1876; Unknown
Ocean Park Library 2601 Main St.	May 3, 1977	Circa 1917; Kegley & Garety, funded by Carnegie
Parkhurst Building 185 Pier Ave.	Dec. 6, 1977	1927; Norman F. Marsh & Co.
First Roy Jones House 2612 Main St.	Jan. 2, 1979	1894; Summer P. Hunt
Horatio West Court 140 Hollister Ave.	Jan. 2, 1979	Circa 1921; Irving Gill
City Hall 1685 Main St.	Oct. 16, 1979	1938; Donald Parkinson & J.M. Estep
California Live Oak Tree 1443 10th St. (Removed, dead)	Jan. 15, 1980	Planted prior to 1900
Marion Davies Estate North Guest House 321 Palisades Beach Rd.	July 17, 1980	1929; Julia Morgan
John W. & Anna George House, 2424 Fourth St.	March 17, 1981	Circa 1911; Unknown
Oregon Ave. Sidewalk Sign west corner of Santa Monica & Fifth	May 20, 1981	Prior to 1912; Unknown
John Byers Office 246 26th St.	March 12, 1982	1926-1954; John Byers
Donald B. Parkinson Home 1605 San Vicente Blvd. (Demolished)	1984	1926; Donald B. Parkinson
Gussie Moran House 1323 Ocean Ave.	Jan. 27, 1987 (On appeal)	Circa 1891; Unknown
Santa Monica Airport Rotating Beacon Tower adjacent to 3223 Douglas Loop	Aug. 11, 1988	1928; Moved to Santa Monica 1952

Nazarene, the Unitrarian Church, the Church of Jesus Christ of Latter Day Saints, the Church of the Foursquare Gospel, and Immanuel Methodist Episcopal Church, which disbanded in the 1950s. Dr. Sue Sikking founded Unity By The Sea in 1944 and conducted services in several buildings before buying the former Evening Outlook building on Fourth at Arizona in 1954. The Santa Monica Westside Council of Churches formed in 1948 and regrouped in 1974 as the Westside Ecumenical Conference, a coalition of Protestant, Catholic, and Jewish congregations.

Those of the Jewish faith were prominent in Santa Monica even before the first lots sold at public auction went to one of the leaders of Southern California's Jewish community, Harris Newmark. Virtually the entire Jewish population of Los Angeles camped out in Santa Monica Canyon or embarked on picnic excursions there to celebrate Jewish holidays. Then, after settlement began, many of the town's first merchants were Jewish. For example, Henry Kowalsky, an eminent San Francisco attorney, purchased the Arcadia Hotel in 1887, only seven months after it was built. Santa Monica's first Jewish religious services were conducted in the summer of 1912 at the Masonic Hall on Marine Street. Although Beth Sholom Temple, Santa Monica's major Jewish congregation, was not built until 1941, Congregation Mishkon Tephilo in Venice served Santa Monica Bay area Jews starting in 1914. A more recent addition is the Chassidic Jewish educational organization, the Bay Cities Chabad House, which began meeting in 1973.

The Self-Realization Fellowship Lake Shrine on Sunset Boulevard near Pacific Coast Highway was opened in 1950. The peaceful 10-acre site includes the Court of Religions, where each of the world's five major religions is represented by a shrine.

The Nichiren Shoshusokagakkai Academy, a large Buddhist organization, established an international headquarters at Wilshire and Sixth in 1975 to coordinate activities of NSA members in more than 30 countries.

PUBLIC LIBRARY

Santa Monica owes its first library to the Women's Christian Temperance Union (WCTU), which established a reading room in 1885. The WCTU solicited contributions of cash and books from the town's leading citizens, and for years organized a variety of library-related fund-raising projects. Under the leadership of WCTU chapter president Jane Austin in 1888, for example, a group of Santa Monica women won a $200 prize for a floral exhibit and were persuaded to donate the entire sum to the library fund. Other fund-raisers included socials, potluck dinners, strawberry festivals, and variety shows.

In 1890 the WCTU donated its entire library, which had grown to about 800 volumes, to the city. The city council appointed a board of library directors which included Lemuel Fisher, publisher of the *Outlook*; Abbot Kinney, real estate developer; and several other leading citizens. The committee rented two rooms in the Bank of Santa Monica and appointed Elfie Mosse librarian. She served in that capacity until her death in 1939.

Next the library expanded to five rooms; then, in March 1903, it was moved to the new City Hall at Fourth and Santa Monica. Through the efforts of many, the Carnegie Corporation was induced to bestow a grant of $12,500 for construction of a library building at Fifth and Oregon (Santa Monica Boulevard). The structure was remodeled in 1927 with the proceeds of a $50,000 city bond issue. The present main library, on Sixth and Santa Monica Boulevard, was built in 1965 and refurbished in 1986. Branch libraries were established in Ocean Park, on Montana Avenue, and in Fairview Heights. The Ocean Park branch, built in 1917 with Carnegie funds and expanded and remodeled in 1986, is the city's oldest

ABOVE: Aviation pioneer Donald Douglas, Sr., established the Douglas Aircraft Company in 1922 at Wilshire and 26th. In 1929 he moved the entire company to Clover Field, where he continued to revolutionize airplane design. Courtesy, Santa Monica Historical Society

ABOVE, RIGHT: The original Douglas plant at Wilshire Boulevard and 26th Street, which used to be an old movie studio, included an aircraft factory and a flying field. It was used from 1922 until 1929, when Donald Douglas moved the company next to Clover Field. Douglas Aircraft built many airplanes for the armed forces and became the city's largest employer throughout the late 1940s and 1950s. Courtesy, Ed Tynan Photo Collection

library building and has been declared a City Landmark.

SANTA MONICA AIRPORT

Santa Monica flew into aviation history with the arrival of the Douglas Aircraft Company in 1922. In his factory at Wilshire and 26th, Donald Douglas built the Douglas DT, soon to be known as the Douglas World Cruiser. From Clover Field, then little more than a dusty runway carved from a barley field, Douglas in 1924 sent four "World Cruisers" on the first round-the-world flight; two made the trip successfully. In 1929 Douglas moved his entire company to the Clover Field site, which it occupied until the 1970s. Douglas then designed and built a prototypical airliner, the DC-1, in 1933. The next year he started building and selling DC-2s, which carried 14 passengers and were the fastest and most luxurious planes in the world. He sold 31 of the 156 DC-2s he turned out to Trans World Airlines (TWA), which inaugurated transcontinental air passenger service in 1935.

Douglas' triumph led to the DC-3, which went into production in 1935. Including its military version, the famed C-47 "Gooney Bird," Douglas built 10,600 DC-3s by the time production ended in 1945. Hundreds of these aircraft are still in service throughout the world.

As a result of Douglas' achievements, Clover Field became widely known to aviators of all kinds. Barnstormers and stunt pilots flew out of Clover, and many of Hollywood's legendary fliers, from Howard Hughes to Hal Roach, based their personal aircraft there. In 1927 William Wyler used the field to film *Wings*, his chronicle of life and death in the skies over France during World War I. Buddy Rogers and Clara Bow starred; the stunt flying was done by a young lieutenant named Curtis LeMay, who went on to become U.S. Air Force Chief of Staff.

During World War II Douglas Aircraft turned out hundreds of A-20 light bombers from its Santa Monica plant. The company merged with McDonnell Aircraft in 1967 and relocated its headquarters in Long Beach. But Clover Field, now called Santa Monica Airport, remains in service.

In August 1988 the last surviving DC-2, a former Pan American aircraft which also saw service in the national airlines of Mexico and Guatemala, was restored to flying condition and re-created TWA's 1935 inaugural flight from Los Angeles to St. Louis.

In 1987 a $20-million overhaul of Santa Monica Airport was begun. The centerpiece of the new airport complex is the $3-million Donald W. Douglas Museum, scheduled for completion in 1989. On display are the memorabilia of Donald Douglas, Sr., and several vintage aircraft, including the last surviving DC-2, a 1930s British Spitfire, a P-51 Mustang, and a DC-3.

THE OUTLOOK

The first issue of the *Outlook* rolled off the press October 13, 1875. Publisher Lemuel Fisher, who had more courage and faith in the future than he did capital, became the new community's most ardent and outspoken booster. When the long battle over the site of the Port of Los Angeles was resolved, however, the meagerly financed news-

BELOW: One of the four Douglas World Cruisers is pictured here just before taking off on the round-the-world flight from Clover Field in Santa Monica on March 17, 1924. Two planes completed the trip, returning to Clover Field six months and 28,000 miles later. Courtesy, Santa Monica Historical Society

ABOVE: The first national home for veterans west of the Rockies was founded in 1888 on land donated by Senator John P. Jones and Arcadia de Baker. Initially named the National Home for Disabled Volunteer Soldiers (nicknamed the Soldiers Home), it became the Veterans Administration in 1930. Pictured here in 1892, the complex included military-style barracks, mess halls, and recreation centers, as well as a theater, library, and chapel. Courtesy, Veterans Administration Archives

RIGHT: The old Santa Monica City Hall, located near Fourth Street and Santa Monica Boulevard, served the city from 1902 to 1938. Today's City Hall on Main Street replaced this earlier structure in 1939. Courtesy, Santa Monica Historical Society

paper was one of the first casualties of the business bust that followed. Fisher thus suspended publication on December 19, 1878, and was unable to resume until January 5, 1887.

Then in 1894 Ellis Woodward purchased the publication; he sold it to D.G. Holt two years later. Holt turned the weekly into a daily, and as such the *Outlook* has continued without interruption. After several more changes in ownership the paper was acquired by its present owners, the Copley organization. On the *Outlook*'s pages (accessible on microfilm at public libraries) are chronicled, rich in detail, the people and events that compose Santa Monica's colorful history.

SOLDIERS HOME

In 1887 the directors of the National Home for Disabled Veterans began looking for a West Coast site on which to build a major new facility. Some 61 proposed sites, including one on Catalina Island, were considered.

In concert with the owners of the Wolfskill tract, adjacent to the old Rancho San Vicente y Santa Monica, John P. Jones and

Arcadia de Baker offered a 300-acre site near what is now Wilshire and Federal. In November 1887 the government formally accepted the site for the Soldiers Home.

Another 200 acres were later added to the property from Jones' and Baker's holdings, deeded from their Santa Monica Land and Water Company, and a military cemetery, second only to the one at Arlington, Virginia, was established to the east of the Home on land deeded by the Wolfskill family.

The Soldiers Home was a collection of military-style barracks, mess halls, recreation, administration, and service buildings—including a theater, chapel, and library—all constructed in the grand Victorian style. Water was piped in from the nearby springs. The first resident, Private George Davis, was admitted on May 2, 1888. By the end of the year the first barrack was completed and settled with retired soldiers, most of them veterans of the Indian Wars or of the Civil War.

As the Home filled with residents, company from all over the country came to visit with their kin. To provide hotel rooms, restaurants, and shops for these visitors, the town of Sawtelle sprang up along the Home's south side.

By 1897 the Home was largely self-sufficient, raising its own livestock, grain, vegetables, and several kinds of fruit. By the turn of the century the complex had its own steam and electrical generators. Additional buildings were added over the decades; Wadsworth Hospital, south of Wilshire Boulevard, was built in 1927 with annexes added during World War II and in 1959. The last of the original structures was razed in 1957.

Today the entire complex, including a modern hospital with a large neuropsychiatric facility, is administered by the Veterans Administration. The hospital has enjoyed a long and close relationship with the medical school at the nearby University of California, Los Angeles.

Locations

Bundy Pumping Station is located at 1228 South Bundy Drive. Site of the old Santa Monica Water Company, the station continues to supply much of the city's water. Bundy Drive, named after pioneer George Bundy, meanders because it follows the path of an old creek bed, which dried up once the wells that fed it were diverted to the city's water supply.

Santa Monica Hospital, at 16th and Arizona, remains on the site purchased by Doctors Mortensen and Hromadka in 1925. It is widely regarded as one of the region's most modern facilities.

St. John's Hospital & Health Center stands at 1328 22nd Street. It serves both Santa Monica and West Los Angeles. Over the last several decades it has become known as the "Hospital of the Stars" because so many film celebrities have sought treatment there.

City Hall, on Main Street between Colorado and Pico boulevards, was designed by local architects Donald Parkinson and J.M. Estep and built in 1938. It forms part of a complex that includes city and county courts, the Santa Monica Police Department, and other civic offices, and is a City Landmark.

Rapp Saloon, at 1438 Second Street, is the oldest masonry building in the city. Built as a beer garden in 1875, it was used as the Town Hall between 1887 and 1889.

Methodist Episcopal Church building, begun in 1875, was the first church constructed in Santa Monica. Located at 2621 Second Street and now a private residence, it is a City Landmark.

Public Library, at 1343 Sixth Street, continues to serve all of Santa Monica. The central library is widely admired for its reference and periodical collections, while the refurbished library building has become a center for community activities.

CHAPTER FIVE

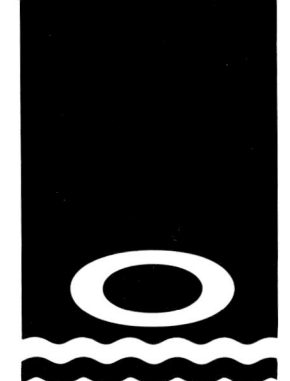

Re-drawing the Map

Authentic Italian gondoliers, flower-lined walks, and buildings designed in the style of the Italian Renaissance helped to fulfill Abbot Kinney's dream of a Venice in America. Courtesy, Santa Monica Historical Society

OCEAN PARK

World traveler, noted conservationist, political heavyweight, champion of Indian rights, and art connoisseur, wealthy beyond imagine from the manufacture of Sweet Caporal cigarettes, Abbot Kinney was raised in the East, came to San Francisco in 1880, then settled in Sierra Madre. In 1886 he put together a land development syndicate, purchased acreage on the north side of Santa Monica Canyon (later sold to the Southern Pacific as part of the Long Wharf project), and moved into a home along Ocean Avenue, near the sea air.

Kinney soon became a power in Santa Monica affairs as a member of the Library Commission, the Casino tennis club, and as road commissioner. In 1891 he and partner Francis Ryan (father of tennis champion Bunny Ryan) bought the sandy strip south of the city limits, renamed it Ocean Park, and began building cottages and leasing lots. Roads were laid out; parks, pavilions, and piers were constructed. In addition,

73

Afternoon strollers and local fishermen enjoy the first Ocean Park pier in 1897. Courtesy, The Getty Center for the History of Art and the Humanities, Los Angeles, California

New Jersey native Abbot Kinney established the early community of Ocean Park, but soon turned his attention to the tidewater marshes south of Santa Monica, in pursuit of his dream to build a Venice in America, complete with canals, gondoliers, and Renaissance architecture. Courtesy, Santa Monica Historical Society

Kinney persuaded the YMCA to site its summer home at beachside. Soon Ocean Park attracted other developers, including the always industrious Vawters, father and sons.

For decades Ocean Park was "the other side of the tracks," in this case the Southern Pacific tracks that ran along what is now Colorado Avenue. Nevertheless, under relentless development, Ocean Park beat Santa Monica to the bathhouse boom by opening such an establishment before Santa Monica did. Moreover, Kinney and Ryan built a race track and a golf course, and arranged to buy water from the City Water Company, which pumped it from wells on property owned by William Vawter.

In 1900 there was talk in Ocean Park of secession from Santa Monica, but when put to a vote the measure lost, 341 to 59. In 1901 M.H. Sherman and Eli P. Clark's electric trolley line, the South Loop, was extended to the section of Ocean Park to be known later as Venice, bringing with it

ABOVE: Ocean Park Bank on Pier Avenue is pictured here on a sunny afternoon in the early 1920s. Courtesy, Ed Tynan Photo Collection

LEFT: Townspeople of Ocean Park, dressed in their finest, stroll along Pier Avenue on this busy day in the early 1900s. Courtesy, Santa Monica Historical Society

RIGHT: Employees of the Abbot Kinney Company, which developed much of Ocean Park and Venice, stood in line near Marine Street for this Fourth of July photo, circa 1920. Courtesy, Santa Monica Historical Society

FACING PAGE: A large crowd milled about on the rebuilt Ocean Park Pier on this delightful day in 1927. Among some of the amusements shown here are the spiralling 150-foot lighthouse slide (center), the High Boy roller coaster (right), and the Egyptian Ballroom (back). Courtesy, Elliott Welsh

This elaborate 2,600-seat auditorium graced the end of the Venice pier. Built in 1905, the hall showcased lectures, sporting events, symphonic concerts, plays, and many other cultural events. Sarah Bernhardt was one of many celebrities to perform on this stage. Courtesy, Santa Monica Historical Society

hordes of beachgoers. Thus the pier complex and surrounding amusement zone prospered.

Kinney next persuaded the U.S. Postmaster to establish the Ocean Park post office, so that Santa Monica had two facilities with different names, an unusual event in that day. In 1902 the *Ocean Park Review*, a weekly newspaper, began publication.

In 1904 the secessionists won a partial victory when the southern portion of Ocean Park incorporated as an independent city.

Seven years later, under Kinney's influence, the City of Ocean Park became a sixth-class city, Venice. The northern part, which maintained allegiance to the City of Santa Monica, comprises what today is known as Ocean Park.

VENICE

Abbot Kinney had been intimately involved in the development of Ocean Park, but he had still grander visions. In 1902 he abruptly sold half his interests and looked southward—toward the tidewater marshes of old Rancho Ballona, where hunters stalked the wily mallard, coot, and teal; where fishermen prowled in flat-bottomed skiffs; and where none but the webfooted dared to live. As Kinney looked toward this swamp of desolation, he envisioned an American Renaissance budding in a new city. In his mind's eye, Kinney saw rising from the muck and bulrushes the domes and arches of a new Venice, complete with canals and gondoliers, a center for the arts and letters, a setting to inspire the fullest measure of creative talent from the young and vigorous Americans who would settle there. And he set out to make his dream a

RE-DRAWING THE MAP 77

Abbot Kinney, the primary developer of the Venice community, poses outside his wood-framed family home with his wife, Winifred, and their two children, Helen and Thornton. Courtesy, Santa Monica Historical Society

The southern portion of Ocean Park, which included Abbot Kinney's Venice of America project, incorporated as a city in 1904. Because the northern portion of Ocean Park was still a part of Santa Monica, growing confusion over the new community's name prompted the City of Ocean Park to change its name to Venice in 1911. Courtesy, Los Angeles Public Library

reality.

In 1892 Kinney had persuaded the Santa Fe Railroad to build tracks northward from Port Ballona, in order that construction materials and equipment—and, later, passengers—could be brought to the site where his dream Venice would rise from the swamps. Two noted architects, Norman Marsh and C.H. Russell, were commissioned to give this dream of Kinney's concrete form.

By 1904 men and mules were mucking about, building canals to drain the swamps. Kinney enthusiastically promoted the new settlement, persuading many of Santa Monica's merchants, restauranteurs, and hoteliers to put up buildings in a style which recalled the Italian Renaissance. Thanks to Kinney's wealth, fame, and connections, news of the new beach resort and arts center spread around the world.

Meanwhile, the canals were laced with

LEFT: The many derricks of the Venice oil field are pictured here in 1930, looking toward the 43rd Street bridge. Courtesy, California Historical Society/Ticor Title Insurance, Los Angeles

graceful bridges; gondolas were brought in to serve as taxis. Some 17,000 electric lights were installed, modern illumination on a scale never before seen in the West. Flower beds bursting with color lined the streets, and small parks dotted the town.

At the end of Windward Avenue, Kinney built a pier, to which concessionaires added roller coasters, rides, and amusements. Nearby was built a 2,600-seat auditorium, reckoned by many to be the finest such facility on the West Coast. On its stage performed such luminaries as the incomparable Sarah Bernhardt.

In addition, Kinney planned art festivals and a plethora of other cultural events. Thus to Venice flocked thousands of visitors, who drank and danced in the Venetian Gardens, sunned and sailed and strolled the beaches, played tennis, dipped in the ocean, or crowded the pier to observe yacht races. Several grand hotels, including the St. Mark's and the Cabrillo, which was built in the manner of a ship, offered luxurious accommodations to visitors from all over the world.

While many remained skeptical of this American Venice, others became swept up in Kinney's grand vision. Land values boomed, stirred by speculators, and construction of homes and office buildings continued, nonstop, for months. Then, on July 4, 1905, 40,000 visitors came to see for themselves. Entertained by orchestras, speeches, and fireworks on the lagoon, the crowds witnessed the most magical day in Venice's history.

In his haste to create a miraculously modern, medievally-inspired mecca, Kinney's engineering plans were lacking in depth. So were the canals, which had served to drain the swamp but had then ended up as four-foot-deep ditches with unlined and uncompacted bottoms. With merely one water gate to the sea, tidal action failed to scour pollution from the 16 miles of uniformly level ditches. These soon began to silt up; in a few years they had become festering open sewers. By 1912 the State Board of Health had declared them menaces to public health.

Moreover, like much of Southern California, Venice suffered from an acute potable water shortage. In the early 1920s, when Los Angeles acquired the rights to a seemingly unlimited supply of Owens Valley water, the thirsty communities of Santa Monica Bay requested a share. The price, however, was annexation. Santa Monica declined, and by turning to the mountains for spring water and digging wells, the city maintained its independence. Venice, though, had no such assets. Faced with no other choice, Kinney's vision in 1925 became one

This aerial view shows the Venice of America of Abbot Kinney's plans—canals with bridges, streets, and shop fronts in the architectural style of old Venice. Due to poor planning, the canals ended up as four-foot-deep ditches and were ultimately declared a public health menace in 1912. Many of the canals were filled in and paved as streets, though some waterways still remain today. Courtesy, The Carrillo Family

Locations

Ocean View Hotel, 1513 Pacific Avenue, Venice, was where controversial evangelist Aimee Semple McPherson spent her last night on May 18, 1926, before disappearing from the beach in a kidnapping hoax—enabling her to be with her lover out of public view.

Venice Canals can be viewed best from near Washington Boulevard and Pacific Avenue. Only a skeletal grid of the canals remains.

Boardwalk spans the beachfront from Rose Avenue south to Washington Street. The wooden slats have been replaced with concrete.

Neilson Way, just east of the beach in Ocean Park, is the former trolley route from Santa Monica to Venice boulevards.

Crystal Beach, at the foot of Hollister Avenue, is the site of the Crystal Pier, which was torn down in 1949.

Marine Street Telephone Exchange, at Neilson and Barnard Way, was built in 1926. This is the last remaining original building in Santa Monica's Ocean Park redevelopment area.

Mendotta Block, 2667 Main, is owned by Bill Cosby. This was one of the first commercial structures in Ocean Park.

ABOVE, RIGHT: The charming oceanfront walk, which spanned the shoreline from Ocean Park to Venice, is still a popular attraction today. Looking north from the Venice area, the Ocean Park Pier and the Egyptian Ballroom are visible in this early 1900s view. Note the style of the streetlights, which lined the center of the walkway. Courtesy, Dr. Robert Weinstein

more suburb of Los Angeles. Two years later most of the canals were filled in and paved over as streets; a few still remain as testament to Kinney's soaring imagination.

In the 1930s Venice's fortunes declined with the discovery of oil under its tidewater lands. Unsightly derricks sprang up everywhere, and the town became tarnished with the effluvia of storage tanks and wellheads. While the boom lasted only about a year, hundreds of residents lost their savings or their land after borrowing to invest in drilling wells on their property. The derricks were finally removed during the 1960s and 1970s.

In the 1970s, when roller skating became a fad, Venice enjoyed a revival as a recreation spot. Skate shops opened their doors to thousands of weekend visitors. The beachfront boardwalk was transformed into a combination free-for-all roller derby and swimsuit exhibition. Skaters of all sizes, races, and sexual persuasions, sporting a panoply of colorful costumes, danced to raucous outpourings from boom boxes. Fortune tellers, jugglers, acrobats, and street musicians roamed the area. In the 1980s the boardwalk remains popular as an open-air bazaar for seekers of souvenirs, sun glasses, stylish casual clothing, and scrumptious food.

Today Venice is undergoing urban renewal as businesses move into renovated or rebuilt structures and as population pressure from Los Angeles and Santa Monica draws young, upwardly mobile residents. This same pressure has also brought an influx of homeless people, who camped out on beaches during the winter of 1987-1988 to the dismay of property owners.

Yet, however tardily, Abbot Kinney's vision for Venice has begun to be fulfilled. A bond issue was passed in 1987 to fund canal cleanup. Meanwhile, crowds jam weekly into the Beyond Baroque Foundation for readings by renowned poets. Artists and musicians have settled in large numbers along the newly landscaped canals. And Venetians have made a virtue out of the dearth of available parking to walk or cycle around town, thus lending the community a welcome Old World atmosphere and an air of sunny liberty.

Lofty palm trees along the Santa Monica coastline are silhouetted against a lavender sky. Photo by Justine Hill

LEFT: The carnival rides at the base of the Santa Monica Pier are a popular attraction for the area's residents as well as visitors from neighboring communities. Photo by Patty Salkeld

TOP: The restored antique carousel on the Santa Monica Pier enchants and delights both children and adults with its colorful charm and hand-carved wooden horses. Photo by Justine Hill

ABOVE: The entrance to the exciting Santa Monica Pier is located at the foot of Colorado Boulevard. Photo by Patty Salkeld

ABOVE: Many vivid images are created by the setting sun along Santa Monica's coastline. Photo by Paul Morse

ABOVE, RIGHT: Palisades Park is an ideal location for a leisurely stroll, a brisk run, or some quiet time in the sun. Photo by Justine Hill

RIGHT: A solitary windsurfer skims along the ocean water in the late afternoon shadows of Malibu's green hills. Photo by Patty Salkeld

ABOVE: Colorful boats, picket fences, and brilliant flowers create many graphic scenes along the canals of Venice. Photo by Patty Salkeld

LEFT: Colorful beachfront walks teem with activity year-round. Photo by Patty Salkeld

TOP: This dynamic mural animates Ocean Park Boulevard near the corner of Main Street. Photo by Patty Salkeld

ABOVE: Santa Monica Place, bordered by Broadway, Colorado Avenue, Fourth, and Second, is the city's largest enclosed mall with more than 150 stores. Photo by Paul Morse

CHAPTER SIX

The Provinces

MALIBU

Between Santa Monica and Ventura lies a narrow strip of sandy beaches, rocky coves, misty mountains, and hidden canyons—home, before the coming of the white man, to Chumash Indian villages such as Sequit and Malibu. The entire Chumash territory extended from Morro Bay in the north to Las Flores Canyon, just west of Big Rock.

The Chumash were kin to the Yuman, who lived near present-day San Diego. Between their territories, in what are now Orange and Los Angeles counties, lived the Shoshonean-speaking Gabrieleños, whose ancestors had invaded from Utah and Nevada.

In 1542 pine-planked Chumash canoes decorated with red paint and sea shells greeted Cabrillo and his caravels. Juan Rodríguez Cabrillo paused briefly to note the peaceful encounter, yet with little interest in the area's wild canyons and wave-washed beaches he sailed on without coming ashore. Sebastian Vizcaino, 60 years later,

Even in the mid-1920s traffic sometimes clogged the old Coast Road, now known as Pacific Coast Highway, as beachgoers made their way to the sand and surf along the Malibu area coastline. Courtesy, Ed Tynan Photo Collection

89

was of similar mind. Gaspar de Portolá and Juan Bautista de Anza, traveling by land, sensibly avoided the region's sheer cliffs and steep mountains.

Thus the Malibu, as it came to be called, remained wilderness well into the nineteenth century. In 1805 the Spanish governor of California granted Malibu to Don José Bartolemeo Tapia, although Bartolo, as he was known, never got around to recording the deed. That was left to his heirs, who took possession after his death in 1824. The deed was then finally registered in the name of Maria Tapia, Don José's widow, in 1845, and Tiburcio Tapia, their son, became executor of the estate.

Tiburcio Tapia was one of the leading men of his era, a heroic soldier and successful merchant. By his middle years, in fact, he was more than merely rich. He also found time for civic responsibilities: he served three terms as alcalde for Los Angeles, twice as legislative representative to the newly independent Mexican nation, and also as a member of the Los Angeles police commission, as recorder and as a judge.

In addition, Tapia had an interest in Rancho Cucamonga. Thus, in the 1840s, as he and other Californios began to sense American ambition in annexing California, Tapia became anxious about his cash. According to family legend, he buried several trunks of silver and gold coins in secret places on the Cucamonga and Malibu ranchos. Tapia died in 1845—and his treasure remains where he buried it, somewhere in Malibu.

Wild and remote, the Malibu meanwhile was a haven for smugglers and bandits. In 1819, for example, a smuggler's ship was lured ashore by Antonio Briones and Maximo Alanis, two hitherto respectable landowners, who tricked the smugglers into putting their goods ashore, then threatened to turn the loot over to authorities unless the smugglers paid ransom. While negotiations were in progress, the smugglers escaped, and Briones and Alanis scooped up the goods and fled. Somehow customs authorities were alerted, and the two landowners were arrested and the smuggled goods confiscated. Briones and Alanis spent six months chained in a dungeon.

Horse and cattle thieves also found sanctuary in the Malibu wilderness. Ironically, following the American annexation of California, many of those arrested in the Malibu bore the name Tapia, cousins and nephews of the great Don Tiburcio.

In 1848 the Malibu was sold to Leon Prudhomme, 26, a naturalized American of French birth, and to his bride, 16-year-old Maria Merced Tapia, Tiburcio's daughter. But in 1852, when the new American Land Commission began confirming—or denying—Spanish and Mexican land grants, Prudhomme was unable to prove ownership. Nowhere could proof be found that the Tapias ever held proper title to the Malibu. Thus in 1854 the commission rejected Prudhomme's claim. Although he appealed the decision, as the case dragged on he ran out of money and energy; moreover, his attorney was less than able. Finally, in 1857, Prudhomme threw in the towel. He sold Malibu to Don Mateo Keller for 10 cents an acre.

Don Mateo, né Matthew, was a shrewd, seminary-educated Irishman who had come to Mexico and thence to Los Angeles around 1850. Keller planted vineyards along Alameda Street and soon became king of California's winemakers. He imported orange seedlings from Central America to start a nursery and grew cotton and tobacco. Keller, a Mason and noted musician, also joined the Vigilance Committee, a self-styled posse formed to protect merchants against the rowdy, wicked den of thieves that terrorized early Los Angeles. In addition, he helped organize a volunteer fire company. And when land prices fell after the Gold Rush petered out, he speculated in land.

In 1863 Keller went into Federal District Court, obtained a decree substituting himself for Leon Prudhomme, and appealed the failed claim for ownership of the Malibu.

With the help of "new evidence," a sharp attorney, and a court considerably more liberal than that of the previous decade, Keller got clear title to the Malibu's 13,315 acres.

Don Mateo, who was otherwise busy with partners founding the Pioneer Oil Company and, with Phineas Banning, the Los Angeles & San Pedro Railroad, did little to improve the Malibu. He built some corrals and a few buildings, including a ranch home of rock in Sostern Canyon. Then when he died, in 1881, he left the property to his son, Henry. In 1891 Henry sold it for $10 an acre to Frederick Rindge.

Rindge came out from New England in 1887, a 30-year-old with Puritan ancestors and a puritanical outlook. With $2 million inherited from his wool merchant father, Rindge quickly became a force in the community. He built a home for his bride, Rhoda May Knight, at Ocean and Wilshire, and sponsored construction of Santa Monica's first city hall and first library.

Rindge's Malibu Ranch was to become his idyllic retreat. He built a grand home complete with lavishly landscaped grounds and a gurgling fountain; he added a barn, bunkhouses, and corrals, and he stocked his spread with lambs, pigs, chickens, ducks, geese, and a solitary peacock. In the fertile coastal valleys he planted rippling fields of grain; cattle grazed in the grasslands. He built dams and roads and planted lemon orchards.

To accommodate travelers who sometimes crossed his ranch on their way up or down the coast, Rindge also built two bunkhouses. One was neat and clean, the other dirty and infested with lice and other vermin. He bunked uninvited guests according to his notion of their integrity; honest wayfarers got clean bunks, while those he suspected of being bandits, highwaymen, or fugitives spent the night scratching lice. Opium smugglers continued to use Paradise Cove and Point Dume's beaches; one night Rindge hosted a band of detectives who had come to spy on suspected smugglers. Ironically, though Rindge was a fervent supporter of the temperance movement during Prohibition, bootleggers would use these same places to bring ashore contraband liquor.

As further indication of his hospitality, Rindge would host autumn rodeos on his ranch. He envisioned the time when Malibu would become a sort of New World Riviera, dotted with expansive homes and traversed by an inviting road connecting Santa Monica with Hueneme farther up the coast, thus attracting upscale travelers in fine coaches to enjoy the Malibu's natural wonders.

In 1903, however, a catastrophic fire swept the ranch. Fed by dry chaparral and driven by the wind, in two hours the flames reduced every building in Malibu to embers studded with stone chimneys and hearths. Rindge and his family fled to Santa Monica.

Sam Carson, brother of the famous frontiersman Kit Carson, is pictured here in front of his ramshackle home in Rustic Canyon in the late 1890s; the home is now located in Topanga State Park. Courtesy, Santa Monica Historical Society

The U.S. Mail stage is pictured here circa 1910 in the Topanga Canyon area of Malibu. Courtesy, Santa Monica Historical Society

The Methodist Episcopal Church built their Pacific Coast Chautauqua Camp in the Pacific Palisades in 1921. The camp's meeting house, which also served as a library, is pictured on the right. Small cabins or "casitas," used for housing, can be seen to the left. Courtesy, Santa Monica Land and Water Company Archives

Then, in 1905, Rindge, only 48, died after a brief illness. His widow, May, resisted the inducements of land developers and fought to keep the ranch intact. It was a decision that would cost her dearly.

Homesteaders on land abutting Malibu steadily increased in number. Many trespassed to gain access to water or to graze livestock. As people crowded into Southern California, the Malibu's empty interior appeared increasingly more attractive. Land developers greedily eyed the Malibu.

The Hueneme & Malibu & Port Los Angeles Railroad, presided over by May Rindge, was used to ship grain and hides. However, pressures for commercial roads continued. Farmers and ranchers still needed to cross the Malibu to take crops and livestock to market, to bring in supplies, and to seek work in the cities. On horseback or in wagons, they traversed ranch roads, often without permission, sometimes camping along the way. Mysterious brush fires and lost livestock marked their passage.

Finally, in 1908 the County of Los Angeles proposed a road through the ranch to the Ventura County line. But the Queen of the Malibu, as May Rindge came to be known, ignored court injunctions to open her roads. In 1917 she put up high fences along ranch boundaries. Her armed riders repulsed travelers and even lawmen seeking to serve papers.

The state then took over the court battle. Six years and a king's ransom in legal fees later, the U.S. Supreme Court ruled that California's right of eminent domain included the Malibu. Nevertheless, in 1923, engineers escorted by deputy sheriffs were driven off the Malibu at gunpoint by May Rindge's riders.

Then in October 1925 a Superior Court judge gave California the right-of-way to build a highway (now State Highway 1) across the ranch. Judge Frederick Valentine awarded Rindge $107,289 for damages to the ranch; she had asked for $9.18 million. Bulldozers rolled across the Malibu.

May Rindge next began developing the

Santa Monica end of the ranch. She formed the Marblehead Land Company, which started the "movie colony" at Malibu Beach. In short order Hollywood's kings and queens—and robber barons—began leasing beachfront property. To make improvements and speed development, Marblehead sold bonds. Rindge herself sold a section of Las Flores Canyon coastline through a real estate broker; her plan was to use the sale money to retire the bond debt.

Everything went awry, however, when the broker's methods of raising cash were called into question by securities regulators. Thus the property came back to Marblehead, and to save the foundering company Rindge sold off more than one million dollars of her own stock and bond portfolio at bargain-basement Depression prices. It was not enough, though, and in 1935 Malibu went into bankruptcy. To meet expenses, trustees sold off everything on the ranch—until there was nothing but the land itself left to auction. In 1940 Rancho Malibu went on the block to developers.

Fortunately, May Rindge did not live to see the bulldozers turn the wild country of the Malibu into cozy shacks, grand villas, ramshackle beach cottages, shopping centers, office buildings, and such. She died in her West Adams mansion in 1941, all but penniless. Ironically, in 1987 the current owner of the building, an attorney, received an urgent communication from Boston, seeking the whereabouts of Frederick Rindge or his heirs. There was, in a New England bank, a huge inheritance that had gone unclaimed for more than 80 years.

Today Malibu is a bustling community, home to wealthy recluses and ordinary workers, to sparkling shops and seedy eateries alike—a study in contrasts, famous worldwide for its prime surfing beaches and movie star residents. Much of the Malibu's natural beauty remains, though longtime residents, who remember its halcyon days, complain of traffic jams, crowded beaches, and rising crime. As this book goes to press, Malibuans are still grappling with the question of incorporating as a city.

The Santa Monica Land and Water Company Building, pictured here in 1926, was originally built in 1924, and is the oldest commercial structure in Pacific Palisades. Courtesy, Santa Monica Land and Water Company Archives

An adventurous group of professional men and businessmen organized the Uplifters Club, after breaking away from the Los Angeles Athletic Club in 1913. The name of the club was inspired by the uplifting of the arts and the lifting of a cocktail. In addition to the sponsorship of artists and the production of elaborate plays and concerts, the Uplifters built a club polo field in Rustic Canyon, which is pictured here in 1927. Courtesy, Santa Monica Land and Water Company Archives

PACIFIC PALISADES

Above Santa Monica Canyon's sheer cliffs, overlooking the sea, is a narrow mesa—sloping, wild, and secluded—virtually uninhabited until just after World War I. The spot seemed perfectly suited as a meeting place to discuss lofty humanistic and spiritual ideals, so the Southern California Conference of the Methodist Episcopal Church purchased 1,100 acres from the state. Pacific Palisades thus became the site for the Pacific Coast Chautauqua Camp in May 1921.

The following January the town of Pacific Palisades was founded during a meeting under a grove of magnificent oaks. In the decades since, the outlines of the village that sprang up on this mesa have blurred as development has continued. Today, Pacific Palisades is part of the City of Los Angeles. It is generally agreed that the community includes the original town, the populated portions of Santa Monica Canyon, and the coastline north of Santa Monica and south of Malibu.

Meanwhile, back in its early days, the new city lacked retail establishments, so in 1924 construction of a "Business Block" was begun. Then, in 1925, a mining consultant working for Alphonzo Bell discovered rich deposits of limestone, alumina shale, and silica shale—the major components of cement—on Bell's land near Santa Ynez Canyon. Bell, who had developed Bel Air from its pristine state into a secluded showpiece for the wealthy, heard opportunity knocking. In 1928 he petitioned the Los Angeles

These popular beachfront camping facilities in Pacific Palisades, shown here in the mid-1920s, were used by many travelers and tourists, including several local religious organizations. Courtesy, Santa Monica Land and Water Company Archives

Planning Commission for a zoning variance to permit quarrying and construction of a cement plant.

While businessmen were generally supportive, rival developers and many Palisades home owners were opposed, fearing that the solitude and beauty that had attracted them would be imperiled. Thus began a long and bitter battle.

Bell wanted to build 300 miles of roads through the mountains, opening them to further development. His plan called for recontouring and landscaping the excavated areas, and for building small community centers, horse stables, country clubs, a golf course, and a European-style village on the shores of an artificial lake, which would include beaches and a marina. All these attractions were to be connected with landscaped roads and equestrian trails.

Meanwhile, in Los Angeles, the controversy had attracted partisan supporters. William Randolph Hearst's *Examiner* attacked the project; Harrison Gray Otis' *Times*, rarely opposed to any real estate scheme, just as vehemently supported Bell. The result was a tremendous barrage of publicity which served to put Pacific Palisades into the forefront of Southern California's public consciousness.

Finally, after much revision of his original plan, Bell obtained a permit to lay a pipeline under the Coast Highway in December 1928. Even so, fearing last minute objections, his crews stealthily worked through the night to complete the project. This strategy did not endear Bell to his critics,

A gathering of these early automobiles indicates that an event of some import was transpiring on this oceanside bluff in Temescal Canyon in the early 1900s. Courtesy, Santa Monica Historical Society

For many years, the only direct path to the beach for Santa Monica residents was the famed "99 Steps," pictured here in the late 1880s. Courtesy, Santa Monica Historical Society

These actors were photographed while performing a scene for a silent Western on an Inceville movie set in Santa Monica Canyon, circa 1912. Courtesy, Santa Monica Historical Society

however.

Nor did the May 22, 1929, test blast at his quarry site, which had originally intended to demonstrate that such activity would hardly disturb the surrounding countryside. A seismographic crew showed up to monitor the explosion; Bell had them forcibly ejected, injuring, according to some accounts, an elderly scientist.

Finally in early 1930 Bell got his permit to begin full-scale blasting and construction. Yet, before he could begin, opposing forces began referendum proceedings and filed appeals with the California Supreme Court. The court promised a decision by June, but before they could rule, Bell was buried by the consequences of the October 1929 stock market crash.

Cash-poor from margin calls and bank failures, Bell in May sold all his real estate holdings, except Bel Air, for $10 million, at the time the largest real estate deal in Los Angeles history. Then, in June 1931, the newly elected Los Angeles City Council revoked his zoning permit. Today the only part of Bell's vision which remains is a lake in Santa Ynez Canyon, which was created by his earth-moving operation in the canyon below.

Meanwhile, over the years, the Palisades has become a mecca for the affluent, attract-

ing more than its share of those with wonderfully inspired notions. One of the more notable of these residents was Adolph Bernheimer, who in 1924 bought a seven-acre mule camp, where he accommodated drovers and the equipment they used to carve roads into the area. For three years Bernheimer's workers transformed the campgrounds into one of the world's most magnificent gardens. In its heyday Bernheimer Oriental Gardens attracted some 5,000 visitors a week to its elaborate temples, pagodas, lotus ponds, waterfalls, and statuary. Surrounded by lush begonias, lotus blossoms, and fuschias, the gardens were an island of Eastern tranquility. However, a landslide closed the property in 1948, and, except for the remnant of a wall near Marquez Place and Sunset, almost no trace remains.

Since the time of the Chumash and Gabrieleño Indians, who established sacred worship sites in the Palisades canyons, the area has attracted a wide spectrum of religions. After the Methodists came Christian Scientists, Presbyterians, Lutherans, the Calvary Church, a Pentecostal sect, Roman Catholics, Jews, the Latter-day Saints—and the Self-Realization Fellowship, which established a park-like center at Inceville, where filmmaker Thomas Ince shot Westerns.

The Self-Realization Fellowship was established in 1949 by Parmahansa Yoganda, an Indian mystic, along the shore of Bell's artificial lake. It includes a full-scale replica of a sixteenth-century Dutch windmill originally built as the residence of W.E. McElroy, a Twentieth Century Fox set construction superintendent.

On another part of Inceville is the National Center for Transcendental Meditation, founded by Maharishi Mahesh Yogi. The sign greeting visitors reads "Capital of the Age of Enlightenment in California."

Pacific Palisades cemented its place in history in 1980, when Ronald Reagan, a longtime resident of San Onofre Drive, became the 40th president of the United States.

Locations

Will Rogers Home can be visited in Will Rogers State Park, 14253 Sunset Boulevard, Pacific Palisades. Open to the public, it contains mementos of his long career as a writer, wit, showbusiness celebrity, and radio raconteur.

Marquez Family Cemetery lies on the west side of San Lorenzo in the first block north of Entrada, the only lot without a building. Thirty members of the Marquez family, original settlers of Santa Monica Canyon, as well as family servants and friends, including Sam Carson, son of famed Indian fighter Kit Carson, are buried here. The cemetery is closed to the public.

Leo Carrillo State Beach is located at the foot of Decker Road, west of Point Dume. The noted actor, for whom the beach is named and who lived in Santa Monica Canyon, donated the land so that the public could enjoy the Malibu's oceanfront.

Serra Retreat, at the top of Serra Road, Malibu, is now owned by the Franciscans and named for Father Junipero Serra, founder of the California missions. Most of the original structure was destroyed by fire in 1970; the present building, erected in 1974, includes a remnant of the Malibu Ranch home built by Mrs. Frederick Rindge.

Keller's Shelter is a cove to the east of the Malibu Pier. Don Mateo Keller's boats were often anchored here.

Malibu Colony lies in front of Malibu Center. The colony's residents, including many famous film stars, guard their privacy with security gates and armed patrols.

Getty Museum is located at 17985 Pacific Coast Highway. The original museum was part of J. Paul Getty's residence; "The Richest Man in the World" filled it with art masterpieces. In 1974 the present museum, just downhill from the original, was opened to the public. It is a reconstruction of an authentic Roman villa excavated at Herculaneum (near Pompeii) which was buried by an eruption of Mount Vesuvius in A.D. 79.

CHAPTER SEVEN

Partners in Progress

As could be expected for a beachfront community located in a warm and sunny climate, tourism led to Santa Monica's earliest commercial ventures, more than a century ago. As the railroads completed their move westward, more and more easterners were lured to Southern California by reports of warm days, cool evenings, and Pacific Ocean breezes.

As do so many other California communities, the name Santa Monica reflects the Roman Catholicism of the early Spanish explorers and settlers. An early Santa Monica resident and keen student of California history, Charles A. Tegner, found the first local references to what would become the City of Santa Monica to be Boca de Santa Monica and Rancho San Vicente y Santa Monica.

The rancho was acquired in 1872 by Colonel Robert S. Baker, who, two years later, sold 75 percent of his interest to Senator John P. Jones of Nevada. The latter immediately laid out a townsite. Tegner wrote of it: "A marvel city named Santa Monica by the owners of this townsite, and probably after the name of the great rancho they were subdividing."

The first business established in the community was a grocery store, opened to serve the many visitors flocking to the beaches. Then came a hotel, the first of many, followed by a commercial wharf. As soon as the townsite was laid out in 1875, the real estate business began flourishing. Within a year the town boasted some 1,000 residents and more new enterprises, including a newspaper, *The Outlook*.

Not long after the start of the twentieth century, Santa Monica had become a thriving residential community. Meeting the needs of a growing population meant providing goods and services, and before long there were financial institutions, insurance and real estate firms, restaurants, churches, schools, and hospitals.

World War I and the Great Depression brought some struggles, but Santa Monica continued to grow, while retaining its character as a pleasant beachfront community. Then came the 1940s and the outbreak of World War II. The war economy brought many changes. Douglas Aircraft, a local company, became a major military supplier and employed thousands of workers. By the time the war was over, Santa Monica was a bustling city.

Today that city continues to grow and prosper. Somehow it has managed to retain its seaside ambience while continuing its economic progress. Much of the credit for that happy combination belongs to the organizations whose stories are told on the following pages. Their support of this important literary and civic project is a reflection of their pride in the community's progress.

Five hearty surfers pose with their boards on Santa Monica's beach in the 1930s, with the California Incline visible in the background. Note the wood surfboards, which at that time measured 14 to 18 feet and weighed about 150 pounds. Courtesy, Santa Monica Land and Water Company Archives

SANTA MONICA HISTORICAL SOCIETY

The Santa Monica Historical Society was founded in 1975 by the City of Santa Monica Centennial Committee, chaired by Aubrey E. Austin, Jr. Mrs. Ron Funk was the society's organizing chairman, and former Mayor Clo Hoover became its first president. Designated as the caretaker of Santa Monica's history for the benefit of future generations, its motto is, appropriately, "Preserving the Past."

The historical society now has more than 400 members of diverse ages and backgrounds, including descendants of land grant holders and pioneers, as well as businesses and other organizations representing all segments of the community. In 1982 the 300-member Santa Monica Pioneer Society, founded some 80 years ago, merged with the historical society, creating a broader base of support.

The nonprofit historical society operates, on behalf of all citizens of the Santa Monica Bay area, for the advancement of historic information and for the collection, documentation, and preservation of objects and memorabilia relating to the Santa Monica-Westside area dating back to Indian times, up through the periods of Spanish, Mexican, and, finally, United States rule.

A major goal achieved by the society, spearheaded by Louise Gabriel with the support of the board of directors, is the founding of its Museum of History and Culture. It houses the Westside's largest collection of Santa Monica area memorabilia and artifacts, some of which date back to the 1800s. Centrally located on Colorado Avenue at 20th Street, this multidisciplinary museum contains a reference library, photographic archive, exhibition gallery, an audiovisual theater, vintage clothing, and an ever-expanding collection of historic artifacts and memorabilia. The society already has more than 6,000 photographs of Santa Monica's early days and close to 7,000 rare books in its collection.

Among the many community activities conducted by the historical society are the annual Pioneer Picnic, art poster and essay contests for schoolchildren, tours of sites and landmarks, and commemorative celebrations for local and national occasions. Many of the society's members worked on the city's Centennial Committee in 1975. Other commemorative events held by the society included a tribute to Douglas Aircraft founder Donald Douglas, a city hall ceremony on the occasion of Santa Monica's 110th birthday in 1985, and the four-year-long celebration of the bicentennial of the United States Constitution. The society works to preserve landmarks and was in the forefront of a six-year campaign to save Santa Monica's oldest building, the landmark Rapp Saloon, from demolition.

In 1984 the society, with the co-sponsorship of the City of Santa Monica and the Bandini families and friends, installed a monument in the Rose Garden of Palisades Park honoring Arcadia Bandini de Baker, wife of Santa Monica co-founder Colonel Robert S. Baker. During her lifetime she and the other co-founder of the city, Senator John P. Jones, had contributed a great deal of land for churches, parks, schools, and other community uses. It was the first time she had been so honored; Senator Jones had previously received tributes. The society, with UCLA and Steven Spencer, cosponsored an archaeological dig in Santa Monica that revealed 3,000 pieces of artifacts from the late 1800s and early 1900s reflecting the middle-class lifestyle of the period.

Through efforts such as these, plus its publications, including *Santa Monica—Jewel of the Sunset Bay*; educational programs; exhibitions; speakers' bureau; workshops; and seminars, the dedicated volunteers of the Santa Monica Historical Society are very effectively preserving the past for future generations.

Joining in the ribbon cutting ceremony on October 8, 1988, for the grand opening of the Santa Monica Historical Society Museum of History and Culture are (from left) Charlotte Bossel, president, Soroptimist International, Santa Monica; Kay Collins, president, Santa Monica Independent Insurance Agents Association; Clarita Marquez Young; Kathy Lennon; Laura Blosdale; Andrew Calkins Carrillo, Historical Society president; Virginia Tegner Spurgin; Herb Katz, Santa Monica mayor pro-tem; Mary Lee Gray, senior deputy for Deane Dana, Los Angeles County Board of Supervisors; Louise Gabriel, past president, founder/organizer of the museum; Jack Siegal, president K-SURF Radio; former Santa Monica mayor Clo Hoover; Dave Paradis, executive director Santa Monica Area Chamber of Commerce.

MONTANA AVENUE AND ITS MERCHANTS' ASSOCIATION

When Senator John P. Jones of Nevada acquired a majority interest in the land on which Santa Monica was to be built, he had a townsite drawn up in 1874. The northern boundary was Montana Avenue, running from the Pacific Ocean to 17th Street.

In the more than a century since that time, as Santa Monica has grown and changed, Montana Avenue has grown and changed with it. Primarily a residential street at first, it retains much of that flavor, although a large portion east of Seventh Street is now commercial. Some of the earliest merchants ran blacksmith shops, which were replaced by gas stations, which eventually gave way to a mixture of service-oriented and upscale retail establishments that make up much of today's business population.

Yet not everything has changed along Montana Avenue. The building at the southwest corner of Lincoln Avenue has always housed a pharmacy, and the Aero Theatre, at 1328 Montana, has been in operation since the 1920s. Carl's Bakery, Le Petit Moulin restaurant, and the Esquire Barber Shop have been operating since the 1930s, and most of the original buildings still stand. The dean of Montana Avenue Merchants is Frank Moody, who has operated Moody Printing on Montana since 1942.

Today the section of Montana Avenue running from Seventh to 17th streets marks the territory covered by the Montana Avenue Merchants' Association. The organization was formed years ago by a group of concerned shop owners and operators whose primary goal was to sponsor and promote events that would foster a spirit of cohesiveness between residents and merchants.

In May of every year the association sponsors a sidewalk sale, with a portion of the proceeds used to help support Stepping Stone, a local crisis center for homeless and abused youth. As much as $10,000 has been raised in a single year.

On the first weekend of December the merchants hold open house, as street decorations go up, and Santa Claus and strolling carolers greet residents and shoppers. The association also sponsors poster contests for local schoolchildren on such subjects as safety. Posters are displayed in shop windows all along the avenue. In July the Annual Santa Monica Bed Race, sponsored by Kiwanis for the benefit of the Santa Monica Chapter of the American Red Cross, is held on Montana Avenue, between Seventh and Ninth streets.

The organization, which is headed by a chairman, vice-chairman, secretary, and treasurer, aided by an advisory board that includes about a dozen block captains, holds some eight meetings per year to plan its various events and to keep members posted on issues affecting them. A directory of the more than 200 merchants and professionals on the street is published periodically. Montana Avenue is part of a business assessment district, and the association uses a portion of the funds from that source for group advertising.

There is a great deal of pride along Montana Avenue, among residents, landlords, and merchants alike. Many of the buildings, some lovingly restored, have been in the same families for generations. No structure is more than two stories high, and landscaping abounds. Merchants, most of whom are Santa Monica residents themselves, are quick to refer customers to one another. Many of the shops are owned and operated by women, and there is a strong emphasis on both visible ownership and personal service.

All along Montana Avenue the atmosphere is that of a friendly neighborhood, providing the clearest evidence that the Montana Avenue Merchants' Association is successful.

TOP: These three buildings on Seventh and Montana were owned by the same family for 66 years and were sold to the Montana Avenue Preservation Company, with Steven Soboroff as managing general partner.

BOTTOM: This is the same block shown after major renovation and restoration. Carl's bakery and Le Petit Moulin, both of which had been in this building for more than 40 years, today remain operating in the new project. Keeping long-standing neighborhood businesses preserved is a priority to many of the property owners.

CENTURY WEST DEVELOPMENT, INC.

In its corporate brochure, Century West Development, Inc., describes itself as "a fully integrated real estate development firm offering a unique ability to minimize risks, obtain excellent financing, and provide reasonable profits through the development of premier projects in prime locations." Its clients can be found throughout the United States and within the Pacific Rim region.

Despite its broad scope, Century West is very much a Santa Monica company, and not simply because it is headquartered there. Century West's ties to the community run deep, historically and philosophically. In the words of board chairman and chief executive officer C.C. "Harry" Mow, "We're a very locally oriented company, and we understand the goals of the city's leaders and its people. We build projects that blend in with the community, that enhance the general quality of life here, and that foster creative and productive long-term working environments."

Locally, the firm's projects include the 45,000-square-foot Portofino Plaza, located across the street from the Pacific Ocean at Santa Monica Boulevard, where its corporate headquarters is housed. Other Santa Monica projects are the Pacific Gardens, which is an 88-room retirement hotel; the Santa Monica Medical Building; Palisades Promenade; and Santa Monica Square.

Historically, the ties also run deep. Although Century West itself was founded in March 1979, the involvement of its principals in Santa Monica began much earlier. One of its founders, William E. Cook, is in fact a Santa Monica native who, prior to the formation of Century, operated William Cook Development, Inc., specializing in building multifamily residential units.

In 1976 two aerospace engineers from the Santa Monica-based Rand Corporation, John Dudzinsky and Harry Mow, became involved in Cook projects, primarily as investors. With a third engineer, John H. Yueh, Mow and Dudzinsky formed MYD and Associates and, with Cook, were developing six or seven projects per year by 1978 on a joint-venture basis.

The early success of these ventures caused Mow, who had been program director of Advanced Technology at Rand, to resign in January 1978 in order to run the MYD partnership interests. A year later Cook and the MYD partners decided to formally join forces, and Century West Development, Inc., was born. Today the company is managed by Mow as chief executive officer; Dudzinsky, who is president; Cook, chief operating officer; and Kenneth G. Walker, executive vice-president. Yueh retired from the firm in 1985.

Century West enjoyed early success, and by 1980 the staff

ABOVE: The partners of Century West (from left) are John Dudzinsky, president; Kenneth G. Walker, executive vice-president; C.C. "Harry" Mow, chief executive officer; and William E. Cook, chief operating officer.

BELOW FROM LEFT TO RIGHT:

A future Century West development, the Palisades Promenade will be located at Ocean and Broadway.

This 16-unit apartment building in West Los Angeles is a Century West development.

The Bugle Boy Industry headquarters, located in Chatsworth, California, is a Century West project.

numbered 45. In 1981 the firm launched its first commercial project, a 72,000-square-foot office building at 201 Santa Monica Boulevard. Then a recession hit the real estate industry, and by 1983 the company's staff had been reduced to 11.

That was the low point, however, and the firm has grown steadily ever since. It now employs more than 70 people on a full-time basis and builds an average of 30 projects per year. This includes about 500 units of apartments and 200,000 square feet of office buildings, generating from $70 million to $80 million in annual revenues. The company is closely held, with the principals owning most of the stock and the balance held by senior staff members.

Before arriving in Santa Monica in 1963 to join Rand, Mow had spent most of his life in New York. Born in China, he came to the United States with his family when his father was appointed to represent the Republic of China at the United Nations. He received his doctoral degree in mechanical engineering from Rensselaer Polytechnic Institute in New York.

Dudzinsky, who was with Rand from 1965 to 1979, most recently as program director of Technology Applications, received his doctoral degree in electrical engineering from Carnegie-Mellon University. Cook, who studied business and architectural design at California State University, Northridge, had formed his own development and construction company in 1968. The fourth member of the management team, Ken Walker, has a strong background in finance; before joining Century West, he was vice-president of a major savings and loan association.

Every Century West project is approached with the same philosophy: careful research prior to implementation, followed by hands-on attention to even the smallest detail, every step of the way. A full-service company, Century West handles the most complex construction programs, from land acquisition to complete turnkey projects, including conceptual development, master planning, architectural and interior design, financing, construction supervision, and property management.

This philosophy, coupled with the ability to consistently maintain high returns, has enabled Century West to rapidly broaden its base and has created the firm's history of long-standing client relationships. During

TOP: Santa Monica Square, a business center/ office complex, is located at 201 Santa Monica Boulevard.

BOTTOM: The impressive 45,000-square-foot Portofino Plaza (another Century West project), at 1401 Ocean Avenue, across the street from the Pacific Ocean, houses the corporate headquarters of Century West.

its first 10 years of operation, the company developed more than 140 apartment complexes and nearly one million square feet of office space. The five-year period from 1984 to 1988 saw commercial construction more than double, multifamily residential construction increase nearly tenfold, and total construction volume jump from less than $15 million to more than $75 million annually.

The people of Century West Development, Inc., have reason to be proud of their record—and of their many contributions that have indeed, in the words of Harry Mow, "enhanced the quality of life" in Santa Monica.

CROSSROADS SCHOOL

Crossroads School is different—decidedly so. The difference is expressed in a variety of ways and is most evident in its philosophy of education and in its 21st Street campus, where its classes for students in grades 7 through 12 are conducted. Kindergarten through sixth-grade students attend the Fourth Street location, which was once St. Augustine By-The-Sea Episcopal School.

The 1714-21st Street location is in the heart of an industrial section bordered by Olympic Boulevard and the Santa Monica Freeway. It has been described by even its staunchest supporters as unsightly, weird, ugly, and funky. A *Los Angeles Times* article quoted one observer as saying that the school "has all the ambience of a tire warehouse." It's a campus that, in the words of headmaster Dr. Paul F. Cummins, is "as much a serendipity as a plan."

The first building was acquired not long after the school began operating in 1970. It was considered at first as a temporary site, housing seventh-, eighth-, and ninth-grade classes. However, as a new grade was added each year, more space was needed, and the school acquired a second building across the alley from the first.

The advantages of the location soon became clear. It was a melting pot campus, flanked by both wealthy and poor neighborhoods, and that fit in perfectly with the philosophy of Crossroads' founders that, "Through our academic and extracurricular programs, Crossroads School seeks to promote social, political, and moral understanding, and to instill in students a respect for the humanity and ecology of the earth.

"We understand that there are many kinds of intelligence, and the traditional academic, cognitive area is one. Other important areas of intelligence are intuition, imagination, artistic creativity, physical expression and performance, sensitivity to others, and self-understanding. To neglect any of these areas is to limit students in the development of their full human potential.

"We believe the uniqueness of children is revealed in their very existence, and it is the school's responsibility to foster their innate sense of the mystery and joy of life." Based on its record, Crossroads School has fulfilled that responsibility well. From the beginning, Crossroads sought to develop a diverse student population. To this end, the school has committed 10 percent or more of its annual budget (kindergarten through grade 12) to financial aid, enabling it to provide a quality education to children from all spectra of society.

Dr. Cummins was headmaster/executive director of St. Augustine By-The-Sea School when the parents of some of his students approached him in 1970 about a place to send their children after completing sixth grade, the highest level the school had then offered. The decision was made to start a new school, and in September 1971 Crossroads School for Arts & Sciences opened, with classes for seventh and eighth graders and a plan to add one new class each year, up through grade 12. The nucleus of the student body was from St. Augustine. Dr. Rhoda Makoff, assistant to Dr. Cummins at

TOP: *Crossroads School graduate Aeri Lee, headmaster Paul F. Cummins, and former board of trustees president Nat Trives.*

BOTTOM: *Paul F. Cummins (right), receiving the Exemplary School Award from the U.S. Department of Education.*

Crossroads School "alley."

that school, became Crossroads' first director.

Three years later, when Makoff chose to step aside, Cummins became headmaster at both schools, remaining in those posts until the merger of St. Augustine's and Crossroads in 1982, when he took on his present position.

A native of Chicago, Illinois, Cummins has lived in Southern California for most of his life. A graduate of North Hollywood's Harvard School, he received his bachelor's degree from Stanford University, has master's degrees from both Harvard University and the University of Southern California, and earned his Ph.D. at the latter institution.

The founders of Crossroads School began with five basic commitments: to academic excellence; to the arts; to the greater community; to the development of a student population of social, economic, and racial diversity; and to the development of each student's full human potential. By these yardsticks, and virtually any other one could apply, the school has been extremely successful.

Two of those added yardsticks are supplied by Cummins himself: "Good programs attract good kids;" and "Kids do best when they're happy." Believing that the right atmosphere is more important than competition, there are no letter grades at kindergarten through the eighth grade. The dress code is strictly casual, befitting the 21st Street campus, a facility that now includes 14 of the 16 buildings on both sides of the alley that runs through this former industrial block.

The school is top-rated academically, and its music program is internationally famous, although it is primarily known for its strong college preparatory program. Virtually all of its graduates go on to higher education, and many of its young musicians, even before graduation, have performed with major philharmonic orchestras, including those of New York and Los Angeles.

In 1984 the U.S. Department of Education designated Crossroads School, which now has more than 630 students in its grades 7 through 12 program, plus nearly 180 in kindergarten through grade 6, "one of 60 exemplary schools in the United States."

Dr. Cummins' conviction that "kids do best when they're happy" has been proven not only academically and artistically, but athletically as well. Sports were never intended to be more than an intramural activity, but a taste for excellence, once acquired, affects all areas of life. For example, the girls' varsity basketball team won 55 league games in a row, and their male counterparts reached the CIF final round six years in a row, winning three and becoming state champions in 1987.

Crossroads' students excel in community service as well. All upper-level students are required to participate, and do so with the same degree of enthusiasm that characterizes all their activities. Crossroads School believes that it has a mission—to provide leadership in elementary and secondary education—and, judging from its results, it is fulfilling this goal.

Crossroads Chamber Orchestra in rehearsal.
Photo by Mary Kate Denny

BOB GABRIEL CO.

"Without the support and interest of its citizens, no community can hope for a better lifestyle or a constant improvement in the happiness and well-being of its people."

This statement appeared in the Santa Monica centennial tabloid in the *Evening Outlook* in 1975 and, like all truisms, it still rings true.

Since 1936 the Bob Gabriel Co. has been serving the personal and business insurance needs of Santa Monica and the surrounding area. The firm also has a real estate and property management department.

Bob Gabriel Co. believes in personalized services and has kept that philosophy in practice for more than five decades. Clients have felt his warm, personal style in a direct way whenever they have needed insurance services. "How can I help you?" is the usual response to a client's call.

In fact, many of the original group of customers have stayed with

The Gabriel Building at 2325 Wilshire Boulevard has been Bob Gabriel Co.'s headquarters and office since 1961.

Bob Gabriel Co., even passing down from generation to generation. There are several cases of families continuing to meet their insurance needs through Bob Gabriel Co. from father to son and daughter. In this modern day of proliferation of computers, it is refreshing to know that personalized attention and concern still not only exist but thrive as hallmarks at the Bob Gabriel Co.

Employees of long standing have enjoyed working with clients and contribute to the long-term relationships that have been acquired over the years. Most of the members of the staff have been associated with Bob Gabriel Co. for many years. Three staff members have enjoyed more than 24 years of service: Joanne Higens, customer service representative; Jean Shannon, bookkeeper; and Tony Veschio, account executive. Not far behind in seniority are son-in-law Pat Potter, account executive and sales manager (18 years), and son Robb Gabriel, manager/real estate and property management (17 years).

As a ship is steered by its captain, the Bob Gabriel Co. business atmosphere was set in true course right from the beginning. In his deep-rooted convictions, Bob's commitment to providing good service to the community is directed not only to his business but also to encouraging fellow workers and others to participate in community projects.

Bob, too, has contributed his time and effort to the growth of the city, as exemplified in his participation in many community activities and professional associations. He has received numerous awards and honors for distinguished services in the field of human relations, including the Humanitarian Award from the Santa Monica Bay Area Chapter of the National Conference of Christians and Jews, the Kiwanis Club's Community Service Award, the Santa Monica Realtors' Citizen of the Year Award, and the Boys Club of America's Medallion for Unusually Devoted Service to Youth.

Presently he serves as chairman of the Santa Monica Convention & Visitors Bureau; vice-chairman and director of the Santa Monica Hospital Medical Center board of trustees; a member of the board of directors of the Santa Monica Medical Center Foundation, Wise Senior Services, and Boys Club of Santa Monica; and as a member of the Santa Monica College Advisory Board.

Past community activities include Santa Monica city councilman,

Louise and Bob Gabriel: "We love this community and have enjoyed being a part of it since 1946."

president of the chamber of commerce, president of the Santa Monica Boys Club, chairman of the Santa Monica Recreation and Parks Commission, president of the Santa Monica Independent Insurance Agents Association, president of Sunrise Optimist Club, and member of the Saint Nicholas Orthodox Cathedral Board of Trustees.

Joe Walling, Wayne Harding, and Bob Gabriel, all former presidents of the Santa Monica Chamber of Commerce, at the Santa Monica Boys Club. Reprinted courtesy of The Outlook.

As president of the Santa Monica Chamber of Commerce, Bob's platform was based on keeping an open mind and spirit of cooperation in keeping the city operating for the good of Santa Monica. In conjunction, he believed that social responsibility must be tempered and balanced with fiscal responsibility.

And right at his side is his wife, Louise, who devotes many hours of her time to community work in Santa Monica. Currently she is president of the Santa Monica Historical Society and past president of the Santa Monica Medical Center Auxiliary, Santa Monica Boys Club Auxiliary, and Santa Monica College Associates. In addition, she has received numerous awards and honors for her distinguished services in human relations.

With Bob's background, it is no wonder that he developed such a strong sense of community spirit.

As a boy of nine he worked in his father's grocery store taking phone orders and then delivered them on his bicycle or in his wagon. Naturally, he developed a strong sense of community awareness. At the age of 15 he was promoted to manager. This experience taught him the importance of service—a lesson that has guided his career ever since. "The best sales pitch you can give is service," he says. Service and community involvement are the main thrust of his company's marketing program.

Gabriel enlisted in the Navy in 1942 while still in college at Michigan State Normal College and was commissioned in 1944 at Columbia University. He served two years in the Pacific Theater during World War II.

Following his release in 1946, Bob earned a bachelor's degree and teaching credential at UCLA. Bob and Louise were married in December 1946. Bob taught school in the Los Angeles and Santa Monica school districts. In 1951 he was recalled for duty in the Korean Conflict. While Bob was in the service, Louise raised two children and worked, saving every penny she could. It was with that savings and a loan from his parents that, in July 1954, Bob acquired an interest in the Zydervelt Insurance Agency, which became the Zydervelt/Gabriel Agency. In January 1955 the agency moved from Pico Boulevard to 26th Street and Wilshire Boulevard. In 1957 Bob bought out his partner, and the firm's present name, Bob Gabriel Co., was adopted. Late in 1961 the firm moved to its current location at 2325 Wilshire Boulevard.

Since 1955 both Bob and his wife have been actively involved in their business and civic matters. Their family now consists of three children, Susan Potter, Robb Gabriel, and Sharyl Szydlik, and two grandchildren, Patrick and Bryan Potter.

Bob sees a bright future for the city of Santa Monica, based on the efforts and interests that have been shown by the community and business members in the past. Bob Gabriel and the Bob Gabriel Co. "care" and, because they "care," will continue to be involved with the city of Santa Monica and its role as a special place in which to live and work.

Bob Gabriel in front of his office, circa 1963.

CHAS. A. TEGNER CO.

The history of the Chas. A. Tegner Co. is, in many ways, synonymous with the history of Santa Monica itself. When founder Charles A. Tegner arrived in Santa Monica in the fall of 1887, there were fewer than 2,000 people in the community.

Tegner was born in Gothenberg, Sweden, in 1866. Following the tradition of his native land, he went to sea as a young man but, while serving aboard a British ship, found conditions so distasteful that he jumped ship in New York harbor. He was 16 years old. Later he joined the thousands of immigrants who were moving westward, and arrived in Santa Monica at the age of 21.

Tegner's first job was at a local vineyard, and he used the money he earned to buy real estate. In 1892 he married and, shortly thereafter, launched a fishing business and opened a grocery store. But the spirit of adventure that had brought him from Sweden to New York and then to California was still strong, and, when news of the Klondike gold strike reached California in 1897, he was on his way to Alaska. During the summer of 1898 he served as a Yukon River pilot, earning enough money to allow him to return to California.

In 1902 he launched the Chas. A. Tegner Co., which is now the oldest firm of its kind and one of the oldest of any kind in Santa Monica. Originally a real estate company, the firm developed many commercial and residential properties in the area. Within 10 years Charles Tegner had become a major force in Santa Monica and was one of its biggest boosters.

When World War I brought a sudden end to the real estate boom, Tegner faced financial uncertainty. A real estate syndicate that he managed was disbanded in 1918, giving him property in lieu of salary, which he ac-

cepted reluctantly. When the boom years returned in the early 1920s, those lots brought him a windfall. But he had learned many valuable lessons, becoming so attuned to economic conditions that he wisely retired from business two months before the 1929 crash.

Several years earlier Chas. A. Tegner Co. had branched out into insurance, an operation headed by Charles' son, Carl E. Tegner, who had joined the company in 1924. He was the second of four children born to Charles and his wife, Emma. Following her death, Tegner married the former Mazie A. Bisenius.

Tegner's other son, Hilding A., and one of his daughters, Thelma B. Schober, also joined the firm, focusing on its real estate activities. The remaining daughter, Edla A. Swinney, was not involved in the family business, although her daughter and son-in-law, Virginia and Charles B. Spurgin, later played active roles.

The firm originally was located at Fourth Street and Santa Monica Boulevard and also was housed for a time at 243 Third Street and 314 Santa Monica Boulevard before moving to its present location at 210 Santa

ABOVE: "Insurance" was the dominant part of the company's signs by the time it moved to this office at 314 Santa Monica Boulevard.

BELOW: In this 1910 photo Charles Tegner is seen standing in the doorway of his office. Some of the signs that were hanging on the walls then remain on display today.

Monica Boulevard roughly a half-century ago.

Following his retirement from the firm, Charles Tegner remained active in the community. A founder and past president of the Santa Monica Pioneer Society, he also served as secretary of the Santa Monica Historical Society and developed a serious interest in the history of both the community and the state of California. He amassed an extensive library of books on California history, and his research on local history led to publication of an article entitled: "Who Named Santa Monica?" He also became a world traveler and had returned from a trip to the West Indies just prior to his death in 1952, at the age of 86.

The retirement of Hilding Tegner signaled the end of the firm's real estate activities, and it focused entirely on insurance. Today the company offers a full line of financial services, including life insurance, property and casualty insurance, pension and profit plans, and annuities.

In 1964 Carl Tegner became partners with his niece's husband, Charles Spurgin, and a third man, Ian M. Grant. Carl retired from the firm in 1973 and died nine years later. During his career, he was extremely active in the community, serving as president of Century Federal Savings and Loan Association, the Santa Monica-Ocean Park Chamber of Commerce, and the Santa Monica Kiwanis Club.

Following Carl Tegner's retirement in 1973, the firm was incorporated as Chas. A. Tegner Co., Incorporated, with Charles Spurgin and Ian Grant as officers, and their wives, Virginia Tegner Spurgin and Phyllis H. Grant, as members of the board of directors. The Spurgins, the last direct links to the founding family, retired in 1981.

Grant, who serves as president and chief executive officer, has continued the tradition of community service established by the Tegner family. He is a past president of the Pacific Palisades Rotary Club and was board chairman of the Pacific Palisades/Malibu YMCA. In

The first office of Chas. A. Tegner Co. was on Fourth Street, at the corner of Santa Monica Boulevard.

addition to Grant, there are two other principals in the company. William D. Aspinwall joined the firm in 1980, followed by David K. Nelson in 1982. Both are currently vice-presidents.

More than a century has passed since a young Swede named Charles Tegner made his way across half the world to Santa Monica. He left an indelible mark on this community. Many of the projects he developed still stand, including the Tegner Building, which houses Henshey's Department Store, a landmark in its own right. When he died, on November 7, 1952, the *Evening Outlook* paid him this tribute: "Arriving in Santa Monica as a penniless Swedish immigrant, Charles Tegner has epitomized the enterprising spirit that has characterized this nation. He saw Santa Monica grow from a town of 1,500 to a city of 71,000. And it is no exaggeration to say that part of this growth was due to his own energy and foresight. Santa Monica joins with his children and countless friends in mourning the passing of a well-loved pioneer."

CENTURY FEDERAL SAVINGS AND LOAN ASSOCIATION

John W. Fisher thought about organizing a building and loan association for several years. The idea began forming when he moved from Oskaloosa, Iowa, where he had been in the lumber business, to Long Beach, California. The year was 1920. He launched a new lumber operation in Long Beach, but sold it in 1923 and moved to Santa Monica, where he bought an existing lumber company. Fisher Lumber Company is still in business at the corner of 16th Street and Olympic Boulevard.

In 1927 his building and loan idea became reality when several friends joined him in organizing Century Building and Loan Association, the first locally owned and managed financial institution in Santa Monica. His associates were J.G. Adams, George N. Swartz, C.W. Adams, and another lumberman, W.A. Hudler. Fisher was named president and Hudler, managing officer. The association opened its doors at 226 Santa Monica Boulevard in March; by the end of the year assets totaled $168,737, and a profit of $308 was posted.

In 1928 Hudler resigned and was replaced on the board of directors and as managing officer by I.F. "Ike" Noxon, who remained in those posts for a quarter-century, until his death in 1953. Carl E. Tegner, a Santa Monica native who owned and operated a successful insurance and real estate business in the community, joined the board in 1930.

The onset of the Great Depression presented a major challenge to the young association. The officers took voluntary salary cuts, and the property owner reduced the rent several times. The rate of interest paid to depositors was lowered, and the association was forced to borrow from the Reconstruction Finance Corporation. The crisis was soon past, however, and Century was able to turn the corner.

In 1933 the association converted to a federal charter, becoming a member of the Federal Home Loan Bank System and joining the Federal Savings and Loan Insurance Corporation. A year later the offices were relocated to 213 Santa Monica Boulevard, and in 1935 the name was changed to Century Federal Savings and Loan Association.

By the end of the 1930s Century had grown substantially, with assets in 1939 exceeding one million dollars, a first for the company. Continued growth dictated another move, this time to 1422 Fourth Street, in 1944. Two years later John Fisher resigned from the association he had founded and was replaced as president by Carl Tegner, who had been on the board for more than 15 years, serving as vice-president since 1939.

The association's rapid growth continued. The $2-million mark in assets was reached in 1946, and five years later it exceeded $5 million.

Carl Tegner was affiliated with Century Federal for more than a half-century, serving as a director, vice-president, president, and chairman of the board.

The Santa Monica main office of Century Federal opened at 501 Santa Monica Boulevard in 1975.

When Noxon died in 1953, Ben R. Parkins, who had been with Century for 14 years, was named to replace him as managing officer. Two years later the association reached the $10-million level in total assets and once again moved its headquarters, this time to 1347 Fifth Street.

The first branch office was opened in 1957 at 11423 Santa Monica Boulevard in West Los Angeles. By the end of the decade total assets had grown to more than $32 million.

Parkins retired in 1965. Named to succeed him was a 15-year veteran at Century, Harry J. Christensen, with the title of executive vice-president and managing officer. Under his management the association reached the $67-million level by 1970 and, two years later, passed the $100-million mark.

In 1974 Century opened branches in Marina del Rey and Placentia, obtained approval for an office in Woodland Hills, and broke ground for a new headquarters building. The

Century Federal Building at 501 Santa Monica Boulevard opened in June 1975.

Carl Tegner remained president of Century until 1976, when he became chairman of the board, a post he held until his death in 1982. Although never an operating officer of the company, he contributed a great deal to its growth and prosperity and was deeply involved in the community. The first president of the Boys Club, he also served as president of the Santa Monica-Ocean Park Chamber of Commerce and the Santa Monica Kiwanis Club.

In January 1976 Robert R. Hield, a veteran of 28 years in the savings and loan industry, joined Century Federal as president and chief executive officer. A California native, he received his bachelor's degree from Pomona College and is a graduate of the Indiana University Graduate School of Savings and Loan.

In March 1983 Century Federal took a giant step, merging with Pasadena Federal Savings and Loan Association, which was founded in 1934. Two of the oldest and strongest federal savings and loan associations in California, they were of comparable size, number of branches, and soundness of assets and reserves.

It was very much a marriage of equals, engineered by Hield and his longtime friend, Kenneth H. Patton, president and chief executive officer of Pasadena Federal, who had discussed the possibility for years. Each institution had a five-man board of directors, four of whom were second-generation directors, and each had several branches, with no two of them in the same community.

It was decided that the merged institution would take the name of the Santa Monica partner, with headquarters in Pasadena. Patton was named chairman and chief executive officer, and Hield became president. All 10 directors joined the new board, with monthly meetings held in Santa Monica and Pasadena on an alternating basis.

The combined assets of the new association amounted to more than

ABOVE: *The office of Century Federal, at 213 Santa Monica Boulevard, in the late 1920s and early 1930s.*

BELOW RIGHT: *Century Federal's current board of directors. Vice-chairman Robert Hield is second from left, and chairman Kenneth Patton is sixth from left.*

$500 million. By 1988 Century Federal Savings and Loan Association had passed the billion-dollar level, with 21 offices in four counties. Patton retired as chief executive officer in 1986, but remains as chairman of the board. Hield succeeded him as chief executive officer, retaining the title of president.

Hield divided his time between the Pasadena headquarters and the Santa Monica main office until he retired as president in January 1989. As did so many others who have served Century Federal over the years, he has given greatly of his time to community activities. He has served as a member of the board of directors of the Santa Monica Chamber of Commerce, is on the advisory boards of both the Santa Monica Boys Club and Santa Monica College, and in July 1988 became president of the Rotary Club of Santa Monica.

Century Federal Savings and Loan Association has enjoyed tremendous growth since its founding in 1927. While its expansion has taken it well beyond the boundaries of this community, it remains very much an important part of Santa Monica, to which it has contributed so much for more than 60 years.

SAINT JOHN'S HOSPITAL AND HEALTH CENTER

Saint John's Hospital and Health Center has been serving Santa Monica and surrounding communities since 1942. But its roots, and those of its founders, go back to a much earlier time—to the middle of the nineteenth century.

It was on November 11, 1858, that a riverboat arrived in the four-year-old Kansas community of Leavenworth. On board was a small group of Catholic Sisters who had come from Tennessee at the behest of their bishop to labor among the people of a territory that was still three years from statehood. They were the Sisters of Charity, who, from their newly established base, would expand to eight other states, Peru, and Bolivia. Hospitals, schools, orphanages, and nurseries for abandoned babies sprang up, as the Sisters brought the message of Christ as tirelessly as the pioneers battled for land.

From the beginning the motto of the Sisters of Charity of Leavenworth has been the closing words of

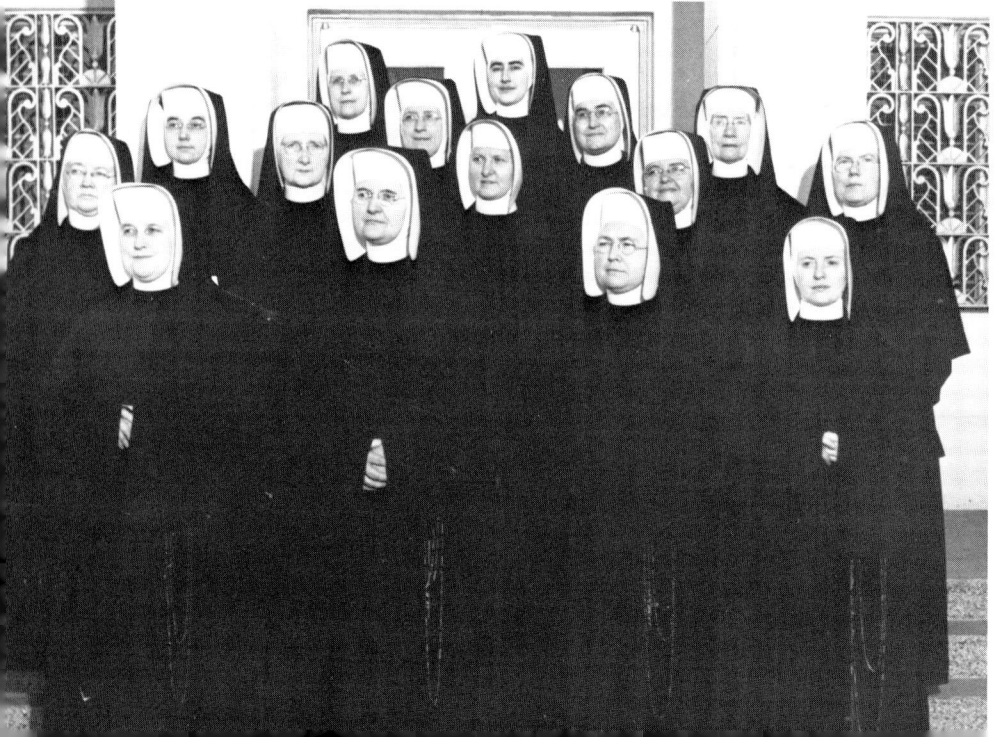

The group of Sisters of Charity of Leavenworth, who came west in 1942 to open Saint John's Hospital.

the 13th chapter of St. Paul's First Epistle to the Corinthians: "... but the greatest of these is charity (love)." For more than 130 years the Sisters have faithfully followed that motto, bringing with them a message of caring, of compassion, of concern.

That message is clearly expressed in the Mission Statement of Saint

One of the Sisters of Charity oversees the construction of Saint John's original facility in 1941.

John's Hospital and Health Center, where it is prominently displayed on a bronze plaque in the lobby. The statement declares that:

Saint John's Hospital and Health Center is a Catholic institution dedicated to creating an environment permeated by Christian values and serving the health needs of people of all creeds, races, colors, sexes, and national origins. We are guided by the philosophy of the Sisters of Charity of Leavenworth, which offers a Christian respect for the integrity of the human person, compassionate concern for human infirmity, and an abiding interest in the care of the whole patient, including his or her spiritual, psychological, and bodily welfare. The living out of these principles includes dedication to the preservation and improvement of human life in all its forms and in all states of development.

Planning for Saint John's Hospital got under way in 1940. A five-acre site on 22nd Street was donated by a group of local doctors, and the construction funds of approximately $750,000 were provided by the Sisters of Charity. Ground breaking for the five-story steel-and-concrete structure took place in May 1941. In October 1942 dedication ceremonies were held, and the following month the first patients were admitted to the 89-bed, 35-bassinet hospital. Waiting to serve them was a medical staff of fewer than 70, supported by some 100 employees.

In its first year of operation the hospital delivered almost 1,700 babies, establishing the first newborn nursery of its kind in Southern California. Later, with the advent of the wartime baby boom, Saint John's built and staffed the first pediatric facility in western Los Angeles County.

Almost from the start the need for health care outstripped the new hospital's facilities. By 1946 an estimated two dozen patients per day were being turned away, and obstetrical facilities had to be reserved six months in advance. An emergency ward and clinic were opened in 1947 and the Sisters immediately undertook major long-range fund-raising campaigns in order to expand the hospital.

In their efforts they were aided by some of the biggest names in the entertainment world, with actress Irene Dunne, later to be called "The First Lady of Saint John's," playing a major role. Others who participated included the brightest names in the Hollywood firmament: Claudette Colbert, Bing Crosby, George Jessel, and Al Jolson, to name just a few.

Construction of a new seven-story North Wing began in 1949, and the first four floors were opened in 1951, increasing the capacity to 225 beds. The top three floors opened in June 1956, adding another 50 beds. The number of physicians on staff exceeded 400, assisted by more than 200 nurses and almost 700 lay employees. Overseeing the entire operation were 20 of the Sisters of Charity, whose love, compassion, administrative skills, and fund-raising abilities were an almost constant source of amazement to the people of the communities they served.

It was at this point that Saint John's became more than a primary service hospital, taking the first steps toward developing into the highly specialized referral hospital and health center it is today. It added elaborate new equipment in virtually all of its departments, offering research opportunities in cancer, protein disturbances, and thyroid disease. A bone and cartilage "bank" for orthopedic work was established, and new services in occupational therapy, cerebral palsy, and psychiatric care were added.

Saint John's Hospital, shortly after its completion in 1942.

The Ross Center, the hospital's mental health facility, was named in honor of Mother Xavier Ross, foundress of the Sisters of Charity of Leavenworth.

The Child Study Center, the construction of which was funded by the Joseph P. Kennedy, Jr., Foundation.

Perhaps the most far-reaching and effective actions at Saint John's were the development of major outpatient and ambulatory care services. Outpatient clinics in psychiatric care, cardiac care, cerebral palsy, glaucoma, dental care, cleft palate, speech therapy, and a well baby clinic were initiated in the early 1950s, often at great personal and financial sacrifice by both physicians and hospital personnel. In 1953, 6,000 patients visited the outpatient service areas at Saint John's. By the mid-1960s that number was approaching 10,000 per year.

In 1960 Saint John's enlarged its already existing service to children with special needs by answering Cardinal McIntyre's request for a facility to assist children with special problems, problems that prevented them from achieving in a regular school setting. With funding from the Joseph P. Kennedy, Jr., Foundation, a building was erected, and in March 1961 the Kennedy Child Study Center was dedicated. In the years since then, the center—now the Child Study Center—has expanded its services and has become recognized as one of the nation's finest centers in its area of specialization.

As the 1960s dawned the hospital was once again bursting at the seams. In 1960 alone almost 1,200 requests for patient admissions had to be refused because of lack of space. A total of 17,000 patients were admitted that year, of which almost 7,000 had major or minor surgery. Close to 20,000 treatments were provided in physical therapy alone.

Among the many volunteer support groups that shared an interest in Saint John's there was great concern. The need for additional facilities was apparent, and plans got under way for construction of a south wing. A key element in that planning was the launching of a major development program. The Saint John's Guild, the Board of Regents, and the Foundation sponsored special fund-raising events, and, for the first time in history, a major motion picture production would provide part of its earnings, and those of its stars, to build a hospital.

When the highly successful *How the West Was Won* was released, its premier showing in Hollywood was dedicated to Saint John's. Through the efforts of its committee, headed by hospital "First Lady" Irene Dunne, more than $4 million was raised for the construction program. In 1967, when the south wing opened, culminating an extraordinary volunteer effort, it included a new 12-room surgery suite, recovery room, laboratory, radiology, cobalt therapy, nuclear medicine, cardiopulmonary laboratory, inhalation therapy, intensive care and coronary care units, and 88 medical-surgical patient rooms.

Still the growth continued. In

Sister Marie Madeleine Shonka, the current president of Saint John's.

1972 an adjacent, privately owned extended services unit was purchased. After a $3.25-million renovation and expansion program, it became the hospital's adult mental health center. Its 87 beds brought the total to 551.

In May 1988 the facility was renamed Ross Center, dedicated to the memory of Mother Xavier Ross, foundress of the Sisters of Charity of Leavenworth. Through the years the Health Center has benefited from the friendship of many area business, civic, and social leaders who formed the Saint John's Hospital and Health Care Center Foundation, the major fund-raising support group connected with the institution. Through them, the tradition of outstanding benefits, including numerous motion picture premiers, continues to bring support for the Health Center's outstanding medical service.

In 1976 the Sisters at Saint John's Hospital and Health Center launched a $12-million, five-year, community-wide campaign for the purpose of completing the new Ambulatory Care Center. Completed and officially dedicated in November 1980, it provided a fully equipped modern facility for such outpatient procedures as lab tests, physical therapy, cardiac rehabilitation, emergency care, and much more.

Caring for little ones has been a primary goal of the Sisters of Charity of Leavenworth for more than a century.

Another five-year campaign, launched in June 1981, raised more than $19 million for remodeling and completion of facilities, major equipment replacement and acquisition, and an endowment for Saint John's Child Study Center. The mid-1980s saw the opening of the Pain Management Center, the Cancer Center, the Heart Institute, and the Post-Coronary Care unit and Saint John's Medical Plaza (1988).

The 1980s also saw the beginning of what has quickly become a Saint John's tradition—The Annual Jimmy Stewart Relay Marathon. Named for the Hollywood legend who regularly participates in a leadership role, the event draws more than 4,000 runners, and the seventh annual race brought in more than $300,000 for the Child Study Center.

For almost a half-century Saint John's Hospital and Health Center has served Santa Monica and its surrounding communities well. It has also distinguished itself as an outstanding corporate citizen. One of Santa Monica's largest employers, with almost 2,000 employees and more than 1,000 physicians, it is assisted in its many activities by 230 volunteers.

The people of Saint John's support numerous community activities, including the Venice Family Clinic, the Senior Health and Peer Counseling Center, the Olive Stone Center, and Turning Point Shelter. Its community education programs include health education forums, health and behavior modification classes, and both community and corporate health fairs. For persons with special needs, such as the chemically dependent, the bereaved, and cancer and AIDS sufferers, Saint John's offers a broad range of support programs.

Today Saint John's Hospital and Health Center, under the leadership of the Sisters of Charity of Leavenworth, continues to demonstrate its faithful adherence to the philosophy expressed in its Mission Statement, offering "a Christian respect for the integrity of the human person, compassionate concern for human infirmity, and an abiding interest in the care of the whole patient."

Saint John's Hospital and Health Center as it appears today.

YE OLDE KING'S HEAD BRITISH PUB & RESTAURANT

Its official name is Ye Olde King's Head British Pub & Restaurant and, while its address is 116 Santa Monica Boulevard in Santa Monica, its heart and soul are as British as Buckingham Palace itself. Stepping across its threshold brings one into an atmosphere more closely akin to Britain than to Southern California.

It was opened in February 1974 by the husband-and-wife team of Philip and Ruth Elwell. A native of Birmingham, England, Phil first came to the United States in 1963 for a visit. Liking what he saw, he decided to move to the United States in 1965. Arriving in California, he worked in banquet sales at the old Ambassador Hotel and then had a small doughnut shop in downtown Los Angeles, which he sold when he opened Ye Olde King's Head.

Now a landmark, it was a small, rundown beer bar in a rundown location when the Elwells first saw it. But they recognized its potential and decided to move ahead. They gutted the facility, redecorating it as an authentic British pub. It was a success right from the start and has never had a negative month. In addition to the bar, they added a small kitchen that only served sandwiches.

As the pub's popularity grew, the Elwells began acquiring adjoining properties, including a Chinese restaurant, a German restaurant, a barber shop, and other businesses. Ye Olde King's Head now occupies what had been seven separate stores. The kitchen was expanded, and both lunch and dinner are now served seven days per week. Restaurant capacity is roughly 150, plus the two bars.

Probably the most popular item on the menu is fish and chips. Customers consume as much as 7,000-plus pounds of cod per month, more than any other outlet in all of California. Other popular items include bangers (always a favorite with the late Cary Grant, who came in frequently), shepherds pie, and midland trifle. The food is so good that the restaurant consistently earns awards of excellence from the California Restaurant Writers Association. Ye Olde King's Head also ranks first in the sale of British beers, offering nine varieties on tap and several other brands in bottles. Phil Elwell is quick to point out that there is a vast difference between a genuine pub and a bar.

The latter is primarily a drinking place, while, for centuries, the pub (an abbreviation for public house) has been the gathering place for generations of Britishers. Traditionally, when new communities are established, the first facilities

TOP: Viscount Althrop, Lady Diana's brother, interviewed Phil for NBC's "The Today Show," and brought an international audience to the pub.

BOTTOM: Ye Olde King's Head British Pub & Restaurant, at 116 Santa Monica Boulevard—an authentic British pub in downtown Santa Monica.

Philip and Ruth Elwell in front of their world-famous Ye Olde King's Head British Pub & Restaurant.

LEFT: The "Taste of L.A." festival brought the King's Head team out in full costume.

RIGHT: Each year Ye Olde King's Head sponsors a cricket match called The King's Head Ashes (Tom Jones' burnt shirt)—patterned after a centuries-old tradition between England and Australia. Ian Botham, a leading British cricket player, was on the team (back row, second from left).

planned are the church, school, post office, and the pub.

The pub was the center of the community, where news and views were exchanged and friendships formed. It was in pubs that such men as Lenin, Marx, Paine, Pepys, and others developed the philosophies that would bring them fame (or infamy).

Ye Olde King's Head is such a place. Virtually all Britishers who come to Southern California include it on their itinerary, and British journalists come in regularly. Whenever British events are in the news, local reporters and newscasters beat a path to the door.

Nor was Cary Grant the only British actor to come in. Virtually all of them have been patrons, and their photos decorate the walls. Ye Olde King's Head has been the setting for many television shows, including an Olivia Newton John special and several episodes of "Charlie's Angels." Led Zeppelin, Supertramp, the Kinks, and many other rock bands have also put in appearances. When Lady Diana's brother Viscount Althrop interviewed Phil for NBC's "The Today Show," Ye Olde King's Head was shown around the world. In addition, Britain's I.T.V. and B.B.C. have helped pass its reputation around the British Commonwealth.

But it has not been just bangers and beer that have made the Elwells' reputation. Their establishment, which is probably the oldest British pub in California under the same ownership, sponsors many other activities designed to keep the traditions of their homeland alive. Each year they sponsor a cricket match called The King's Head Ashes, (Tom Jones' burnt shirt)—patterned after a centuries-old tradition between England and Australia. The event often attracts leading British cricketeers such as Ian Botham.

In the pub itself, of course, there are regulation dart boards. League competitions, tournaments, and championship matches are held regularly. The now-famous Los Angeles Open was conceived there in 1974. The Elwells also sponsor a youth soccer team in far off Auckland, New Zealand.

As visitors from all parts of the British Commonwealth have enjoyed all that Ye Olde King's Head has to offer, they have carried the story back home, helping it develop the international reputation it now enjoys. Not long ago Philip and Ruth Elwell were in a restaurant in Queenstown, New Zealand, waiting for a table, when they were greeted by a married couple who had first met at Ye Olde King's Head.

It has been said that good news travels fast, and that certainly seems to have been true for the Elwells. What began in 1974 as a small British pub with a staff of three has become a major operation with a staff of 65, famous throughout Southern California and wherever the Union Jack is flown.

Lunch and dinner are served seven days per week at the pub, with restaurant capacity at approximately 150 people. Popular and traditional pub grub served at King's Head are bangers, shepherd's pie, and midland trifle.

WHITE & COMPANY INSURANCE, INC.

Ernie White founded the organization that eventually became White & Company Insurance, Inc., March 1, 1952, in Santa Monica. He had just moved from his home in Kansas City, Missouri, after resigning his position as superintendent of agency for the National Life and Accident Insurance Company of Nashville, Tennessee, in its Kansas City, Missouri, office.

White spent the first 14 years of his life on a farm in Kansas and served overseas in the U.S. Army during World War II.

White's first office was a modest one located at 1024 Wilshire Boulevard in Santa Monica. In 1954 the firm moved to a larger office at 1032 Wilshire Boulevard.

From the beginning White pursued an active merger and acquisition policy, whereby the following long-established Santa Monica firms were acquired and/or merged into White & Company.

Due to the acquisitions and the growth of the firm, White constructed a new building and moved the firm in 1962 to 807 Arizona Avenue. On November 1, 1971, the name of the firm was changed from Ernie White Insurance, Inc., to White & Company Insurance, Inc.

Two of Ernie White's three sons, Daryl and Dennis, joined the organization in 1971 and 1972, respectively. A nephew, John Herron, also came on board in 1972. Dennis White is now president, while Daryl White and John Herron are executive vice-presidents. A fourth principal, Andrew Valdivia, joined the agency in 1977 and is now vice-president.

White prefers to focus on the peo-

TOP: *White & Company's first office was at 1024 Wilshire Boulevard.*

BOTTOM: *In 1954 the firm moved to a larger office at 1032 Wilshire Boulevard.*

FIRMS AND FORMER OWNERS	ACQUIRED AND/OR MERGED	ESTABLISHED
Kilgore/Curry Insurance—John Kilgore and Bob Curry	1952	1945
Gandy Insurance—N.S. Gandy and Robert Gandy	1952	1927
Kneeland Insurance— Clifford Kneeland	1955	1944
Bay Insurance—Harry Schroll and Gerald T. McNees	1965	1929
Ira D. Wheeler Insurance—Bob Horrigan	1965	1925
Four-O-One Insurance—First Federal Savings and Loan Association	1971	1940
Kerr Insurance—Alan Kerr	1975	1949

The principals and officers of White & Company Insurance, Inc., are (standing, from left) Bob Horrigan, John Herron, Charles Dunbar, Kevin McMorrow, Jess Williams, Gerald McNees, Kevin Reid, and Andrew Valdiva. Seated (from left) are Jeanne Dahm, Dennis White, Ernie White, Daryl White, and Lillian Urquhart.

ple in the company he founded. He is quick to give the credit for its success to them—not only to the four principals, but to vice-president Jeanne Dahm and company treasurer Lillian Urquhart, who have been with White & Company for 36 and 31 years, respectively. Other officers in the organization who have played an important part in the success of the firm for a number of years are Bob Horrigan, Kevin McMorrow, and Kevin Reid, plus a number of other staff members. Bill Grant (deceased) and retirees Gerald T. McNees, Jess Williams, and Charles Dunbar, former principals and officers, played an important part in the development of White & Company.

Ernie White is especially proud that so many of his staff have been in the organization for 10 years or more and that they have continued the tradition of service to Santa Monica that he established. Community service has long been a hallmark of most, if not all, employees of the firm. Most members have been and are still active leaders in Santa Monica charitable organizations and service clubs.

Ernie White is a past president of several local organizations, including the Santa Monica Chamber of Commerce and the Boys Club of Santa Monica. He has held positions in numerous other organizations, including the Santa Monica Hospital Board of Trustees, Santa Monica College Associates, Santa Monica Community Chest, YMCA and YWCA, United Way, and the American Red Cross. White and other members of the firm have received numerous awards for their civic contributions.

Ernie White became inactive in the management of the company, wanting to pursue his outside interests, which include tennis and traveling. In recent years he has journeyed to such remote parts of the world as Tibet, Mongolia, Bangladesh, New Guinea, and traveled down the Amazon River.

White & Company has now become one of the larger privately held insurance brokerage firms in Southern California with a staff of more than 40. The agency represents many companies writing property and casualty for personal, commercial, and industrial risks. In addition, the corporation has a department handling life, health, hospitalization, and bonds.

In Santa Monica, White & Company Insurance, Inc., is one of, if not the oldest insurance firms under the same ownership.

White & Company Insurance, Inc., now resides in this building at 807 Arizona Avenue.

SANTA MONICA BANK

There are a number of common threads running through the long history of Santa Monica Bank. One is unswerving commitment to quality banking; another is extraordinary community service. Most important of all are the names Austin and Walling—two families who represent more than a century of service to the bank and to the communities it serves.

The story begins on February 17, 1928, when Santa Monica Savings Bank opened its doors. Its founders, all locally prominent businessmen, were Frederick R. Bain, president of the Southern Counties Gas Company of California, who became president of the bank; Aubrey E. Austin, Sr., a partner in the local paving contracting firm of Kneen and Austin,

The first headquarters building was completed in 1938, ten years after the bank opened. It was located at Seventh Street and Santa Monica Boulevard.

Aubrey E. Austin, Sr., one of the original founders of Santa Monica Bank, became president and chairman of the board of the bank in 1933. Aubrey Sr. died in 1949 while still in office.

first vice-president; Max Markowitz, a retired capitalist and realty operator, second vice-president; and Stuart Frazier, manager of the Sierra Bond and Mortgage Company, third vice-president. W.A. Tickle, who had been assistant manager of the Santa Monica office of another bank, was hired as cashier.

The bank's first office was located at Seventh Street and Santa Monica Boulevard. Its mission was to serve the rapidly growing community by encouraging savings and financing residential real estate. From the very first day, the emphasis was on quality.

Santa Monica Savings Bank was less than two years old when the stock market crash of 1929 rocked

the nation. In the ensuing months many banks collapsed, and uncertainty dominated the entire financial industry. But the solid foundation on which Santa Monica Savings Bank was built held firm. Throughout those dark days it was proven to be a solid and secure institution, worthy of the public's confidence.

In 1932 Austin and some of the other original directors and shareholders acquired control of the bank, and the following year he became president and chairman of the board.

Under his leadership the bank implemented a liberal loan policy in response to the needs of the time. It grew rapidly, and in 1933 moved to larger quarters at Fourth Street and Wilshire Boulevard. In 1934 it received its commercial charter and became Santa Monica Commercial and Savings Bank, enabling it to make commercial loans and better serve both the business and residential community. With the region beginning to emerge from the Great Depression, the bank's rapid growth continued. The late 1930s brought another move to larger quarters.

The decision was made to build its own headquarters, and on

February 4, 1938, the newly completed building, at Fourth Street and Arizona Avenue, opened for business.

In 1946 Austin's son, Aubrey E. Jr., was elected to the board of directors and began his full-time career with the bank as assistant cashier in

In 1946 Aubrey E. Austin, Jr., was elected to the board of directors. In 1949 he became vice-president, and two years later he was named president and chief executive officer of the bank. He died in February 1988.

charge of operations and personnel. He had been associated with the banking industry since 1935, starting as a messenger. He was named secretary/treasurer in 1948 and vice-president the following year.

Aubrey E. Austin, Sr., died in 1949, while still in office as president and chairman. He had guided the bank through a period of strong progress and had established a tradition of extensive community involvement. His love for Santa Monica had expressed itself in many areas of service, including the chamber of commerce, the community chest, the Kiwanis Club, and the Salvation Army.

In 1950 Aubrey Austin, Jr., was named president and chief executive officer, and the following year, Joe L. Walling, a 14-year banking veteran, joined the staff as vice-president. Two years later he opened the bank's first branch, in Pacific Palisades.

In 1956 he returned to the main office as executive-vice president and was named to the board of directors. Also appointed to the board in 1956 was another member of the Austin family, Audrey Austin Carver, who had joined the bank a year earlier as head of its public relations department. She remained on the board until her death in 1986, at which time her husband, W. Paul Carver, was elected in her stead.

Under the guidance of Austin and Walling, the bank expanded rapidly and was once again faced with the need for additional space to better serve the needs of its customers. In 1955 plans were drawn for a new structure on the site of the original building at Fourth and Arizona. It opened in October 1956—its 27,000 square feet providing three times the space of its predecessor. A few weeks later the bank opened its second branch, at 33rd Street and Pico Boulevard.

In 1958 the institution officially shortened its name to Santa Monica Bank, by which it had been known for many years.

Austin was named chairman of the board in 1962, retaining the post of president and chief executive officer. That same year the Wilshire-Bundy office was opened. In 1968 the Marina del Rey office was established, and the bank completed its role as a full-service bank by opening a trust department. Another new office, at 23rd Street and Santa Monica Boulevard, opened in 1970.

The bank's Consumer Finance Department, encompassing a new credit card program, was established in 1972. Joe Walling became president in 1975, with Austin remaining as chairman and chief executive officer. Two years later, almost a quarter-century after the two men had begun working together so effectively, their sons, Aubrey L. Austin and Michael L. Walling, joined the staff.

The bank's progress continued, and in 1977 the Edison Company building at 1324 Fifth Street was purchased and became the center for the various operating departments. The main office was enlarged and renovated, and, as Santa Monica Bank celebrated its Golden Anniversary in 1978, it became the largest independent commercial bank on the Westside.

In 1951 Joe L. Walling, a 14-year banking veteran, joined the bank as vice-president. Five years later he was named to the board of directors and in 1975 became president. He succeeded Aubrey E. Austin, Jr., as chairman and chief executive officer in 1988.

The Malibu and Santa Monica Place offices were opened in 1980, and the following year the newly completed Austin Service Center, dedicated to the memory of Aubrey E. Austin, Sr., was opened. By 1988, as the bank celebrated its 60th anniversary, it had grown from a single office with two employees to become one of the 30 largest banks in California and among the top 500 in the United States, with total assets in excess of $600 million.

Santa Monica's long-standing commitment to community service has been a major factor in its success. At every level staff members are involved, following the example set by the Austin and Walling families over six decades. As his father had been, Aubrey E. Austin, Jr., was a major

Aubrey L. Austin represents the third generation of Austins in banking. In 1988 he was named president.

force in numerous organizations. At his death in February 1988, tributes poured in from all across Southern California, and one newspaper called him "The Civic Leader for All Time."

Austin's voluntary activities included banking, civic, fraternal, social, military, and government organizations. Enlisting in the U.S. Army as a private in 1941, he was on active duty for five years, rising to the rank of lieutenant colonel. Between 1953 and 1956 he served as a special assistant, first to the Assistant Secretary of the Army and then to the Under Secretary of the Army.

The organizations that he served as president include the Santa Monica Chamber of Commerce, Santa Monica College Foundation, the Donald Douglas Museum and Library, the Santa Monica Centennial Committee, and the Rotary Club of Santa Monica. He also held leadership posts in dozens of other organizations and received numerous awards, including the Humanitarian Award of the National Conference of Christians and Jews, and was named either Man of the Year or Citizen of the Year by at least a half-dozen groups.

Joe Walling, who became chairman and chief executive officer on the death of his longtime colleague, has an equally distinguished record of community service. He is a past president of the Santa Monica Junior Chamber of Commerce, the Santa Monica Bay Optimist Club, the Pacific Palisades Civic League, the Santa Monica Boys Club, the Independent Bankers Association, the California Bankers Association V, and the Santa Monica Chamber of Commerce.

Walling has also been extremely involved in the activities of the Salvation Army, as members of the Austin family have been. A longtime member of the organization's local advisory board, he served as its chairman for three years and has received

Audrey Austin Carver joined the bank in 1955 as head of its public relations department. In 1956 she was appointed to the board. She remained on the board until her death in 1986.

several awards from the association, including its Sally Award and its most prestigious honor, the William Booth Award. He was instrumental in bringing to completion the Salvation Army's new Santa Monica facilities, dedicated in 1987, having chaired the Building Fund Campaign.

Today, after more than 60 years, the threads that are woven throughout the bank's history are as strong as ever. In 1985 Aubrey L. Austin became a third-generation member of the board of directors. Three years later he was named president. The commitment to quality banking and to community service remain very much in force.

In the Austins and Wallings, Santa Monica Bank has been in good hands for more than six decades, and because of them, Santa Monica has continued to grow and prosper using the philosophy that began in 1928.

K-SURF

Its official name is KSRF, and it is located at 103.1 on the FM dial. But it is more popularly known as K-SURF, The Westside Station. Headquartered in Santa Monica, it serves an area that runs from Malibu in the north to the Palos Verdes Peninsula in the south and from the Pacific Ocean eastward to downtown Los Angeles.

K-SURF first went on the air in November 1960, broadcasting from Pacific Ocean Park, south of Santa Monica. It was founded by George Baron, who had been a salesman for another local station. Other investors were Deane Funk, publisher of *The Outlook*, and John Hearne, who was an attorney with the Federal Communications Commission.

In 1969 the transmitter was moved to the top of the Huntley Hotel on Second Street in Santa Monica and, two years later, to what was then called the GTE Building and is now known as 100 Wilshire. That remains the site of the station's emergency transmitter, the main transmitter having been moved to a ridge on Baldwin Hills in 1985.

On December 15, 1986, K-SURF was purchased by Jack L. Siegal, who put KJOI on the air in 1970 and operated and owned other local stations since that time. During his long and distinguished career, he was a combat correspondent, a radio-TV Navy officer, a reporter-director with Edward R. Murrow's "See It Now," and manager of radio and television activities for IBM, appearing on network television during coverage of both the Gemini and Apollo space missions.

Less than a year after acquiring K-SURF, Siegal bought an Orange County station, KOCM, known as K-OCEAN. Both stations are located at 103.1 on the FM dial and play adult-contemporary music, featuring the hits of the 1970s and 1980s.

Under Siegal's leadership, K-SURF has focused on serving the communities that surround it. Local weather and traffic conditions are aired frequently, and news broadcasts are oriented toward the entertainment industry. The station also does live, on-location broadcasts.

Miss Santa Monica poses in the original glass-walled studios of K-SURF radio station, circa 1961.

Siegal is also responsible for the design of K-SURF's new logo, which is, appropriately, a seagull. The station's hourly identification signal combines the sounds of waves, seagulls, and a foghorn.

K-SURF has established a number of emergency notification systems and it is the official emergency notification station for Santa Monica, Beverly Hills, and Culver City. All pertinent information about an emergency is broadcast at least once every 15 minutes, and there are built-in verification systems between the station and local schools, the police, fire departments, and other groups.

K-SURF was named the Official Radio Station for Beverly Hills' 14-month-long Diamond Jubilee celebration, culminating in 1989. On July 4, 1987, it began what is likely to become a tradition, airing the first "Dawn's Early Light," a 5 a.m. broadcast of Santa Monica's unique early-morning fireworks display. The station's music is synchronized with the fireworks.

K-SURF has become an outstanding citizen of the communities it serves, as has its president and general manager, Jack Siegal. He currently serves on the board of directors of the Santa Monica Chamber of Commerce and the Santa Monica Convention & Visitors Bureau, and on the advisory board of the Santa Monica YMCA, giving of himself, as well as of his business, to the betterment of the community.

KENNEDY-WILSON, INC.

Auction sales have been a common practice for centuries, dating back to at least 500 B.C. In many fields—fine art, thoroughbred horses, tobacco, and other commodities, for example—auctions are the primary means of sale. The sale of real estate via the auction process was often, however, a different matter, usually signaling problems. Often a foreclosure had taken place or the seller needed to raise some quick cash. The auction was typically a matter of last resort.

That is no longer the case. Today real estate auctions have become a well-recognized and accepted means of selling property, especially where large parcels or multiple units are involved. Government agencies, financial institutions, developers, and private companies are now using the auction process with success.

Kennedy-Wilson, Inc., has been a leader in this field since its founding in Santa Monica in 1977 by Don Kennedy and John Wilson. Kennedy, who is still the firm's principal auctioneer, has been in the auction business since 1961 and is regarded as one of the most successful auctioneers in the nation. He served on the Oregon State Board of Auctioneers for eight years, including two as president.

William R. Stevenson, who launched Kennedy-Wilson's real estate operations, bought Wilson's interest not long after the firm's founding and is now its president. Prior to joining the company, Stevenson had many years of experience in various aspects of the real estate profession. He is a graduate of the University of California at Santa Barbara and holds an M.B.A. from the University of Southern California.

Under Stevenson's leadership, the firm has become the largest real estate auction-marketing firm in the nation, having sold close to one billion dollars of real estate by auction throughout the United States. In addition to the Santa Monica headquarters, offices are maintained in Dallas; San Francisco; Phoenix; Portland; Boca Raton; Seattle; Woodbridge, Virginia; and Basking Ridge, New Jersey. As needed, temporary offices are established at major project sites.

Early in 1988 the firm took a giant step forward by joining forces with HSM Group, a fully integrated real estate company involved in all phases of real estate development, marketing, and management. Its partners, Lewis Halpert, Kenneth Stevens, and William McMorrow, join Stevenson as Kennedy-Wilson's four principals. Halpert, with many years of experience in real estate, operated his own successful independent brokerage business, concentrating on

These home buyers attended a scattered-property sale where single-family residences statewide were auctioned.

This dramatic overview shows one of the many properties auctioned by Kennedy-Wilson. These are condominiums in Destin, Florida.

both residential and commercial projects. Stevens, experienced in both project development and marketing, is a former vice-president with Imperial Bank's Real Estate Owned Department. McMorrow, a former executive vice-president of Imperial Bank, was also president and chief executive officer of Home Group Financial Services and executive vice-president of Home Group, a $6-billion NYSE company.

The addition of HSM allowed Kennedy-Wilson to expand its services in property acquisition and management and in traditional real estate sales methods, and to enhance its in-house advertising and other support capabilities. Real estate auctions, however, continue to be the company's primary business, and as many as a dozen projects, involving residential, commercial, or industrial properties; boat slips; raw land; or home sites, may be under way at a given time.

A typical auction-marketing project lasts about four weeks. It begins with an advertising campaign, supplemented by open houses, detailed brochures, and auction catalogs, although no actual selling takes place until auction day. Depending on the project, the auction may attract several thousand people. A few auctions have even been conducted via satellite hookup. One recent auction of 67 units had 800 people in attendance and quickly sold out.

Kennedy-Wilson requires all bidders to register in advance, allowing the company to conduct preliminary credit checks. Once registration is approved, bid numbers and cards are issued. Kennedy-Wilson remains involved in its projects until the close of escrow and endeavors to have backup bids on hand in the event successful bidders are not able to consummate their purchases. In most cases involving residential real estate, the seller will arrange financing for successful bidders. A detailed section on financing appears in every Kennedy-Wilson catalog.

While the typical real estate auction involves only one seller, in 1984 Kennedy-Wilson introduced what it calls scattered-property auc-

Kennedy-Wilson principals are (from left) William Stevenson, Lewis Halpert, Kenneth Stevens, and William McMorrow.

tions and what are often now referred to as "multiple-owner auctions." This process not only affords greater selection for bidders but also allows sellers to reduce their individual promotional costs.

There is no question that auctions have become a major factor in real estate sales, one that is likely to continue growing. "It's a much more open process than one-on-one negotiating," says Stevenson, "and really establishes the true market value of property." He estimates that it will account for about 10 percent of all real estate sales. Others in the industry say that increasing numbers of developers are using auction as their first and only marketing choice.

Stevenson is proud of the role his company has played in upgrading the image of the real estate auction, dealing in prime rather than distressed properties. "We are real estate marketers," he says, "who use an auction at the end of the marketing program. The closing technique is the auction."

Thanks to the pioneering efforts of Kennedy-Wilson, Inc., auction sales have become a fast-growing and highly respected method of marketing real property.

SANTA MONICA HOSPITAL MEDICAL CENTER

Many years ago the following words of Albert Schweitzer were inscribed on the entrance to Santa Monica Hospital Medical Center: "Here, at whatever hour you come, you will find light and help and human kindness." That philosophy has been the motivating force of this hospital since its founding in 1926.

It began with two men—physicians who had been practicing medicine together in Southern California and who saw a need, a need they were determined to fill. Their names were William S. Mortensen and August B. Hromadka, native-born sons of immigrant parents, who had come to Southern California shortly after the turn of the century.

Not long after beginning their respective practices in the Santa Monica area, the two young doctors began helping each other, and in 1918, after Dr. Hromadka returned from military service, they formally entered into a partner relationship. Their practice thrived as Santa Monica grew from 15,000 to 37,000 residents between 1920 and 1930, and more physicians were added to their team.

The rapid growth of the area had severely taxed what limited hospital facilities were available, so Mortensen and Hromadka purchased property at the corner of 16th Street and Arizona Avenue on which to build the first fully equipped and accredited hospital west of Hollywood and downtown Los Angeles. Their efforts to obtain financial support from the community were unproductive, so the two men decided to undertake the project themselves, using their own resources plus funds borrowed from Aubrey Austin, Sr., who would later be one of the founders of Santa Monica Bank.

The new hospital, a three-story concrete-and-brick structure, opened on July 26, 1926. It had 60 patient beds, plus a surgical suite, delivery room, nursery, emergency room, and pharmacy. On the rooftop was an outdoor patio where recuperating patients could enjoy the sunshine and fresh air, while the basement housed a complete physiotherapy unit.

The original staff consisted of some 25 doctors, 10 nurses, an administrator, and a few support personnel. The private room rate was $6 per day; nurses, who worked 12-hour shifts, were paid $75 per month; and tonsillectomies cost $12.50 each.

In building their hospital Mortensen and Hromadka, who owned

The original Santa Monica Hospital in 1926 was a 60-bed facility with three floors and a basement.

Santa Monica Hospital as it appeared in the 1940s. It was a 120-bed hospital then.

60 percent and 40 percent, respectively, had designed the facility for expansion up to a total of 150 beds, never suspecting that even that figure would one day prove woefully inadequate. A 30-bed wing was added in 1928 and another in 1936, bringing capacity to 120 beds. Except for a few lean Depression years, the hospital, which had received accreditation from the American College of Surgeons in 1930, was almost always full, earning a modest profit for its owners.

As the hospital grew, other members of the founding families joined the staff. They included Mortensen's sons, Elmer and William; his son-in-law, Cyril Mitchell; and Hromadka's son, John, all of whom had completed their medical training during the late 1930s and were also in private practice with their older relatives. Another of Hromadka's sons, Ralph, was administrator of the hospital from 1936 to 1966.

The sudden death of August Hromadka in 1939 was a severe blow to the community, the hospital, and especially to his long-term partner. In addition to their hospital responsibilities, the medical practice had continued to grow, and Mortensen was already suffering the early symptoms of a disease that would render him a paraplegic. He semi-retired, leaving the practice in the hands of Elmer Mortensen, Cy Mitchell, and John Hromadka.

Further strain was put on the practice when World War II began, with Cy Mitchell and John Hromadka volunteering for active military duty, serving from 1942 to 1945. The senior Mortensen returned to full-time practice, but soon found that his failing health would not allow him to run the hospital as he had before.

After a great deal of consideration, Mortensen and his late partner's widow decided to donate the hospital to a nonprofit operator; their choice was the Lutheran Hospital Society of Southern California. The transfer was completed on January 4, 1942, with Santa Monica Hospital's value estimated at one million dollars.

Mortensen continued to be involved in the hospital's activities until his death in 1955 and participated in the planning for the

Hospital founders W.S. Mortensen, with shovel, and August B. Hromadka, with sledgehammer, did the ground-breaking honors for expansion of the original facility in 1928.

Celebrities Rita Hayworth and Esther Williams helped raise funds for a hospital expansion project in 1954.

new wing that opened in 1955. That addition increased the facility's capacity to 273 beds. By 1981 capacity had peaked at 399 beds, the majority of them in a nine-story tower constructed in 1971. Today there are 367 beds, reflecting a greater emphasis on outpatient treatment.

Throughout its history innovation has been a hallmark of Santa Monica Hospital Medical Center, at least in part reflecting Hromadka's lifelong interest in the latest medical technologies. For example, he acquired one of the first X-ray machines in the Santa Monica area and brought back the area's first cystoscope from Vienna in the early 1920s.

By the mid-1930s the hospital had an X-ray department, headed by one of the first board-certified specialists, and the most modern radiation therapy equipment available. Doctors Mortensen and Hromadka traveled extensively, attending medical conventions and ever on the lookout for the latest in new technologies. In 1944 the latest "miracle" drug, penicillin, was used at Santa Monica Hospital for the first time, resulting in the rapid cure of a young man who had been close to death.

Other hospital firsts include the first emergency service in the area, the establishment of the first intensive care and coronary care units on the Westside, and the first hemodialysis (artificial kidney) equipment. The hospital pioneered in establishing residency programs in family practice and ongoing paramedic education. The latter resulted in the Nethercutt Emergency Center, constructed in 1969, which is the base station for eight paramedic units serving the Westside communities of Santa Monica, Brentwood, Malibu, and Pacific Palisades. The center is an emergency department approved for pediatrics and certified in first-hour heart care by the American Heart Association.

The Merle Norman Pavilion, which opened in 1986, is the latest addition to Santa Monica Hospital Medical Center. The pavilion features 107 patient beds, a technologically advanced surgical suite with 10 operating rooms, and terraces and courtyards for outdoor convalescing.

Other unique programs include neonatal intensive care, hyperbaric oxygen therapy, osteoporosis detection screening, rape treatment services, computerized physician referral, and in-home health education. The medical staff of roughly 900 physicians represents a cross section of medical and surgical specialties. There are more than 1,400 full- and part-time employees, including 630 health professionals, 300 office workers and clerical staff, 200 service workers, and 190 technicians.

In September 1986 the hospital opened its Merle Norman Pavilion, a six-story tower housing 107 patient beds, two-thirds of which are in private rooms. All patient care floors have direct access to terraces and courtyards, a modern adaptation of the rooftop solarium on the original hospital. The pavilion was funded in

Santa Monica Hospital's nine-story structure on 15th Street, which was completed in phases beginning in 1969, remains an integral part of the medical campus today.

part by Merle Norman Cosmetics, honoring the memory of its late founder.

In addition to the services mentioned earlier, the Santa Monica Hospital Medical Center includes the Children's Dental Clinic; clinical, gastrointestinal, and vascular laboratories; nuclear medicine facilities; orthopedic and pulmonary services; the J. Douglas and Marianne Pardee Oncology Unit; and the Ruggles Ophthalmology Department.

As an integral part of the community, the hospital reaches out beyond medical needs to the mind and spirit of the community by offering a number of additional programs and services. The Les Kelley Family Health Center is an 11,000-square-foot full-service clinic for low-income residents of the Westside. More than 125 physicians on the medical center staff volunteer their time to provide quality medical care. They also share their experiences with the young doctors in the Family Practice Residency Program.

The Volunteer Services Department includes more than 300 volunteers who provide some 80,000 hours of service annually in virtually every department of the hospital. The Lifeline program provides an around-the-clock emergency response service for the elderly and handicapped. The Senior Olympics, sponsored by the medical center, is an annual event drawing more than 200 of the Westside's senior athletes, who compete in track, swimming, and other events. It is just one of several programs focusing on fitness and wellness that the center offers.

The center is fully accredited by the Joint Commission on Accreditation of Hospitals, the American College of Surgeons, and the College of American Pathologists. A teaching hospital, it is affiliated with the UCLA School of Medicine.

Today descendants of the two founding doctors continue to be actively involved. Thomas Soren Mitchell, a grandson of William S. Mortensen, is a physician on staff, and August B. Hromadka's grandson, Donald J. Hromadka, serves on the board of trustees.

At that January 1942 ceremony transferring ownership of the facilities, Mortensen referred to Santa Monica Hospital Medical Center as "a bright and shining name." After more than 60 years of service, it remains exactly that—a place where people "find light and help and human kindness."

KNOLL'S BLACK FOREST INN

Norbert and Hildegard Knoll (the "K" is pronounced) arrived in New York from their native Germany in December 1958. He was from Stuttgart, where his family was in the hotel and restaurant business, and she was from Schwaebisch-Gmuend, in the wine region, near the Black Forest.

A Northern California hotelman had contracted with them to operate a hotel and restaurant for him, but greeted them on their arrival with the news that he had sold out. They took a southbound bus from San Francisco, determined to settle wherever they found a place they liked. That place was Santa Monica.

After working and saving for a year, they opened a small coffee shop at the corner of Second Street and Santa Monica Boulevard. There were eight counter seats and three tiny tables. During the first months of operation as The German Kitchen, the coffee shop served three meals per day, seven days per week. Norbert did the cooking, and Hildegard waited on tables.

From early morning until late at night, the restaurant was immensely popular. The night cleaning crews from the area would arrive for breakfast at 6:30 a.m., followed by the night-shift police officers, and then by the bankers. Later the city leaders, artists, and movie stars would arrive. There was always a wait for tables, and customers would wash dishes and clean tables and counters in order to be seated faster.

After a hectic 18 months the Knolls closed the restaurant for remodeling, reopening as Knoll's Black Forest Inn, with 40 seats. When their son, Ronald, was born, they changed to a schedule of dinner only, five nights per week. Nevertheless, the operation continued to grow, and for 22 years the restaurant, which had expanded several times, was a Santa Monica tradition.

In 1982 the Knolls acquired a facility at 2454 Wilshire Boulevard that had once housed Johnny Sproatt's Bat Rack, a popular restaurant frequented by sports and movie personalities. The Knolls gutted it and redesigned it themselves, in an elegant but comfortable style, with wood paneling, high-backed upholstered chairs, and an enormous collection of beautiful steins and huge cowbells.

Today the capacity is 100 inside the restaurant, plus 85 on the patio. Closed on Mondays, it is open for lunch Tuesday through Friday, and for dinner Tuesday through Sunday.

The Knolls keep as busy as ever. Norbert remains in charge of the kitchen, while Hildegard greets customers in the evening and handles the administration during the day. There is now a staff of 25, plus son Ronald.

The younger Knoll is a UCLA graduate and worked for a restaurant company in Germany before entering the family business, where he helps with the administration while learning all phases of the operation.

Knoll's Black Forest Inn remains as popular as ever. Now, instead of doing dishes, customers can wait in the cozy bar/lounge, which features a fireplace and comfortable sofa groupings.

It has been many years since Norbert and Hildegard Knoll got on that southbound bus, but patrons of the Black Forest Inn should be grateful that it came through Santa Monica and that the Knolls were wise enough to know a good place when they saw it.

Norbert and Hildegard Knoll, both from Germany, arrived in New York in 1958. Settling in Santa Monica, they opened a small, successful coffee shop and 18 months later remodeled and reopened as Knoll's Black Forest Inn. Today the restaurant is located at 2454 Wilshire Boulevard, with a capacity of 100 plus 85 on the patio.

Three views of the interior of Knoll's Black Forest Inn.

The Knolls have been joined by their son Ronald, a UCLA graduate, who is now active in the family business.

THE OUTLOOK

The town of Santa Monica was barely three months old when the first issue of *The Outlook* was published. The date was October 13, 1875. Today *The Outlook* is the oldest newspaper published in Los Angeles County under its original name and the second-oldest newspaper in Southern California.

That first four-page issue, produced in borrowed office space, featured a front-page column by

From this little printshop near the outskirts of the new town of Santa Monica, Lemuel T. Fisher distributed early issues of The Outlook.

founder Lemuel Thomas Fisher that included his reason for choosing the paper's name. "Standing upon the beautiful plateau in front of Santa Monica," he wrote, "looking out upon the broad Pacific, with the mountains and the hills upon either hand and a vast, rich plain stretching to the rear, the thought at once occurred to our mind, what a grand outlook! And we said to ourself, should we ever publish a paper in this embryo city, that should be its name. Contrary to our expectations, we are here, and today we present to the people of this valley, *The Santa Monica Outlook.*"

The first office was in a small wooden building at 1237 Third

Since July 1978 The Outlook *has operated from this building at 1920 Colorado in Santa Monica.*

Street, where the weekly paper was produced for about three years. Then the recession, which had begun in 1877, took its toll. On Christmas Day 1878 Fisher informed his readers that he would "skip a week and take a rest." That "week" turned out to be much longer than expected.

It wasn't until January 5, 1887, that the next issue appeared. It included merely this brief note of explanation from Fisher: "After a little Rip Van Winkle of eight years, *The Outlook* has been revived . . . Its former publisher has returned to his first love." A variety of partners came and went, and Fisher sold his remaining interest in the paper in 1894.

Two years later the paper was changed from a weekly to a daily (except Sunday) and the name became *The Daily Outlook.* The ensuing years brought numerous changes in ownership and in location. By 1929, two years after Ira C. Copley added *The Outlook* to his other newspaper holdings, circulation had grown to 11,000, assets were close to one million dollars, and the paper had moved into a large new facility at Fourth and Broadway.

In 1932 Copley sold the paper to Samuel G. McClure and Jacob D. Funk. It was to be the last ownership change for more than a half-century. Under the leadership of the

The Outlook's emphasis is on local news for the Westside, with all sections of the newspaper carrying stories of local interest.

McClure and Funk families, *The Outlook* continued to grow. By 1960 circulation had climbed to 26,500 and, a decade later, to almost 39,000. *The Outlook* rejoined Copley Newspapers in March 1983 as the 10th member of the La Jolla-based group headed by Helen Copley. Today *The Outlook* publishes two editions daily for its Westside readership.

In 1983 Bertram E. Winrow became publisher of Copley Los Angeles Newspapers, which includes *The Outlook*, the *Daily Breeze* (Torrance), and *The News-Pilot* (San Pedro). Following the tradition established by his predecessors, he has participated actively in numerous professional and community organizations.

Now well into its second century and called *The Outlook*, the newspaper has come a long way since that day in 1875, when a Kentucky-born former Confederate soldier stood gazing at the Pacific and dreamed of launching a newspaper in his adopted community of Santa Monica.

Patrons

The following individuals, companies, and organizations have made a valuable commitment to the quality of this publication. Windsor Publications and the Santa Monica Historical Society gratefully acknowledge their participation in Santa Monica: Jewel of the Sunset Bay.

Century Federal Savings and Loan Association*
Century West Development, Inc.*
Crossroads School*
Bob Gabriel Co.*
Kennedy-Wilson, Inc.*
Knoll's Black Forest Inn*
K-SURF*
Montana Avenue and its Merchants' Association*
The Outlook*
Saint John's Hospital and Health Center*
Santa Monica Bank*
Santa Monica Hospital Medical Center*
Chas. A. Tegner Co.*
White & Company Insurance, Inc.*
Ye Olde King's Head British Pub & Restaurant*

*Partners in Progress of Santa Monica: Jewel of the Sunset Bay. The histories of these companies and organizations appear in Chapter Seven, beginning on page 99.

Students and their teachers were photographed in front of Santa Monica's first public school, which was built in 1876 on land donated by Senator John P. Jones and Colonel Robert S. Baker. Originally named the Jefferson School, this two-story, wood-framed structure soon came to be known as the Sixth Street School. Courtesy, Elliott Welsh

For Further Reading

Armitage, Nora Barclay. *A History of the First Presbyterian Church of Santa Monica*, N.p., n.d.

Basten, Fred E. *Santa Monica Bay: the First 100 Years*. Los Angeles: Douglas-West Publishers, 1974.

———. *Main Street To Malibu*. Santa Monica: Graphics Press, 1980.

———. *Palisades Park Panorama*. Santa Monica: Graphics Press, 1984.

Cleland, Donald M. *History of the Santa Monica Schools, 1876-1951*. Santa Monica Unified School District, 1951.

Cowick, Kate L. *The Outlook's Story of Santa Monica*. Santa Monica: Evening Outlook, 1932.

Crump, Spencer. *Ride The Big Red Cars*. Corona del Mar, Calif.: Trans-Anglo Books, 1962.

Del Zoppo, Annette, and Jeffrey Stanton. *Venice, California*. Venice, Calif.: ABS Publications, 1973.

Edinger, Claudio. *Venice Beach*. New York: Abbeville Press, 1985.

Ingersoll, Luther A. *Century History of the Santa Monica Bay Cities*. Los Angeles: Louis Ingersol, 1908.

Kelsey, Harry. *Juan Rodríguez Cabrillo*. San Marino, Calif.: Huntington Library, 1986.

Lunsford, James W. *Looking At Santa Monica*. Santa Monica: Lunsford, 1983.

Marquez, Daniel Kilgore. *Rancho Boca de Santa Monica*. New York: Vantage Press, 1977.

Marquez, Ernest. *Port Los Angeles, a Phenomenon of the Railroad Era*. San Marino, Calif.: Golden West Books, 1975.

Myers, William A., and Ira L. Swett. *Trolleys to the Surf, the Story of the Los Angeles Pacific Railway*. Glendale, Calif.: Interurbans Publications, 1976.

Mitchell, Thomas S. *Medical Practice in Santa Monica Prior to 1945*. Santa Monica: Mitchell, 1987.

Moran, Tom, and Tom Sewell. *Fantasy by the Sea*. Venice, Calif.: Beyond Baroque Foundation, 1979.

Nadeau, Remi. *City-Makers, the Story of Southern California's First Boom, 1868-1876*. Los Angeles: Trans-Anglo Books, 1965.

Reynolds, Carolyn Covert. *The First 100 Years*. Santa Monica: First Presbyterian Church, n.d.

Robinson, W.W. *Ranchos Become Cities*. Pasadena, Calif.: San Pasqual Press, 1939.

———, and Lawrence Clark Powell. *The Malibu*. Los Angeles: Ward Ritchie Press, 1958.

Smith, Jack. *Jack Smith's Los Angeles*. New York: McGraw-Hill, 1980.

Stanton, Jeffrey. *Venice of America, Coney Island of the Pacific*. Los Angeles: Donahue Publishing, 1987.

Stern, Norton B. *Jews in Early Santa Monica, a Centennial Review*. Los Angeles Jewish Federation Council, 1975.

Storrs, Les. *Santa Monica, Portrait of a City*. Santa Monica Bank, 1974.

Warren, Charles S. *History of the Santa Monica Bay Area*. Santa Monica: A.H. Cawston, 1934.

White, Carl F. *Santa Monica Community Book*. Santa Monica: A.H. Cawston, 1953.

Williams, Barbara. "The Carousel on the Pier." *Merry-Go-Roundup* (10:4).

Wolf, Marvin J., and Katherine Mader. *Fallen Angels*. New York: Facts On File, 1986; Ballantine, 1988.

The Santa Monica Library, shown here in 1912, was first established in a room in the Santa Monica bank in 1890, and moved into its own quarters on Fifth Street and Oregon Avenue (Santa Monica Boulevard) on August 11, 1904. Steel tycoon Andrew Carnegie donated $12,500 for the building after more than 80 citizens collected about $4,000 for the land. The current library is located one block east of this original site. Courtesy, Elliott Welsh

Index

PARTNERS IN PROGRESS INDEX
Century Federal Savings and Loan Association, 110-111
Century West Development, Inc., 102-103
Crossroads School, 104-105
Gabriel Co., Bob, 106-107
Kennedy-Wilson, Inc., 124-125
Knoll's Black Forest Inn, 130
K-SURF, 123
Montana Avenue and its Merchants' Association, 101
The Outlook, 131
Saint John's Hospital and Health Center, 112-115
Santa Monica Bank, 120-122
Santa Monica Historical Society, 100
Santa Monica Hospital Medical Center, 126-129
Tegner Co., Chas. A., 108-109
White & Company Insurance, Inc., 118-119
Ye Olde King's Head British Pub & Restaurant, 116-117

GENERAL INDEX
Italicized numbers indicate illustrations.

Academy of Holy Names, 65
Aguirre, Jose Antonia, 13
"Air Line," 33-34
Alanis, Maximo, 90
Alger, Russell, 32
Alvarado, Juan Bautista, 13
Alvarado, Xavier, 12
American Land Commission, 14-15, 90
Amusement parks, *44, 44-45,* 45, 46, 51, 79
Anderson, Bronco Billy, 44
Anza, Juan Bautista de, 90
Aragon Ballroom, 48, 50-51
Arcadia Hotel, 30, 35, *42,* 44, 54, 67
Arch Rock, *16*
Atchison, Topeka & Santa Fe railroad, 29, 32, 45, 78
Austin, Aubrey Sr., 61
Automobile races, 39, *40*
Aviation, 49, 68-69

Baez, Joan, 48
Baggs, Hamilton Jr., 57
Baker, Arcadia Bandini Stearns de, 18, *19,* 20, 23, 32, 71; sculpture of, *23;* home of, *51*
Baker, Robert S., 16-18, *17,* 19, 20, 23, 25, 26, 27, 38, 44, 62
Ballin, Hugo, 49
Ballona lagoon, 29
Ballona rancho, 13, 15
Bandini, Arcadia. *See* Baker, Arcadia Bandini Stearns de
Bandini, Juan, 18
Bank of Santa Monica, 67
Banning, Phineas, 26-27, 91
Barretto, Maxwell K., 56, *57,* 57-58
Bathhouses, *38, 42, 43,* 44, 54, 74

Baxter, W.O., 55
Bay Cities Chadbad House, 67
Bay City Transit, *34*
Beale, Edward Fitzgerald, 16, 17
Beale, Truxton, 18
Bell, Alphonzo, 94-95, *96*
Berkeley, Samuel L., 57
Bernhardt, Sarah, 79
Bernheimer, Adolph, 97
Bernheimer Oriental Gardens, 97
Beth Sholom Temple, 67
Beyond Baroque Foundation, 80
Bizcailux, Eugene F., 49
Board of Land Commissioners, 14-15, 90
Boardwalk, *4-5,* 80, *80*
Boca de Santa Monica rancho, 15, 16, 21
Bochco, Steven, 49
Breakwater, 32, 51
Brecht, Bertolt, 49
Brice, Fannie, 48
Brighton, "Dad," 58
Briones, Antonio, 90
Bundy, C.L., 21
Bundy, Douglas, *21*
Bundy, Frank, 21
Bundy, George, 21, 57, 71
Bundy, Hallie, *21*
Bundy Drive, 71
Bundy Pumping Station, 71
Byers Office, 66

Cabrillo, Juan Rodriguez, 10, 89
Cabrillo Hotel, 79
California Incline, 26, *98*
Calvary Baptist Church, 65
Camera Obscura, *23,* 23
Cantwell, John J., 61
Canyon School, *62,* 63
Carnegie, Andrew, 133
Carnegie Corporation, 67
Carousel (Santa Monica Pleasure Pier), 46, 51, *83*
Carrillo, Alfredo, 58
Carrillo, Carlos Antonio, 21
Carrillo family, *12*
Carrillo, Jose Raymundo, 12, 21
Carrillo, Josefa Bandini, *21,* 21
Carrillo, Juan J., 21, *38,* 56, *57,* 58
Carrillo, Leopold, 21, *38,* 48, 97
Carrillo, Pedro C., *21,* 21
Carson, Sam, 21, *91*
Carter, William H., 56-57
Casino tennis courts, 38-39
Celebrated residents, 48-49
Cement industry, 94-96
Central Pacific Railroad, 25-26
C-47 "Gooney Bird," 68
Chapin, E.K., 54
Charnock Wells, 59
Chautauquas, *92,* 94
Christian Methodist Episcopal Church, 65
Chumash Indians, 89
Church of Jesus Christ of Latter Day Saints, 67
Church of the Foursquare Gospel, 67
Church of the Nazarene, 65, 67
Churches, 61, 64, 65, 67, 97
City Water Company, 21, 74
Clarendon Hotel, 60
Clark, Eli P., 33, 74
Cleveland, Grover, 32

Clover Field, 68, 69
Cobb, Irvin S., 49
Coffman, H.L., 60
Colored Methodist Episcopal, 65
Congregation Mishkon Tephilo, 67
Cooke & Baker, 16
Cooley, Spade, 50
Copley Newspapers, 70
Cornero, Tony, 39
Cosby, Bill, 80
Craighill Board, 30
Crawford, Joseph, 27
Crespi, Juan, 11
Crocker, Charles, 27
Crothers, Rachel, 49
Crown Point Mine, 20
Crum, John, 65
Crystal Beach, 80
Crystal Pier, 45

Davies, Marion, 48; estate, *50, 51,* 66
Davis, George, 71
DC-1, 68
DC-2, 68-69
DC-3, 68
Deauville club, *36*
Dempsey, Jack, 49
Diebenkorn, Richard, 49
Doeg, Johnnie, 39
Dome pier and theater, 45
Doolittle, Jimmy, 49
Dorton, Randall M., 57
Douglas, Donald W., 49, 68, *68,* 69
Douglas Aircraft Company, 68, *68-69*
Douglas DT, 68
Douglas Museum, 69
Douglas World Cruiser, 68, 69
Duffy, Michael, 44

Earthquake (1933), 64
Echeandia, Jose Maria, 12
Eckert, Robert, 59
Edison Company, 41
Egyptian Ballroom, *80*
Essanay movie studio, 41

Farquhar, Robert David, 51
Film industry, 41, *41,* 44, 96, 97
Fire department, 58-59; station, *58*
Fires, 45, 59, 91
First African Methodist Episcopal Church, 65
First Church of Christ, Scientist, 65
First National Bank of Ocean Park, 21
First National Bank of Santa Monica, 20, 21
First Presbyterian Church, 20, 61, *64,* 65
Fisher, Lemuel, 67, 69, 70
Fisher Lumber Yard, 35
Fitch, Tom, 18-19, 23
Folsom, E.C., 54, 56, 60
Fonda, Jane, 48
Founders Tree, 23
Founding families, 20-21
Francis, Sam, 49
Franciscans, 97
Fraser, Alexander R., 43, 44, 45

Gabrieleno Indians, 10, 89; cooking utensils, *10*
Gambling, 39
Garbo, Greta, 48

134

Garfield School, 63, 64
George House, 66
Getty, J. Paul, 49, 97
Getty Museum, J. Paul, 97
Geuchtwanger, Lion, 49
Geuchtwanger, Marta, 49
Gillette, King, 49
Goldway, Ruth Yannatta, 56
Gomez, Francisco, 11
Grable, Betty, 48
Grofe, Ferde, 49

Hamilton, N.H., 60
Hancock Ranch, 16
Harriman, Edward H., 32-33
Hawe, Patrick, 65
Hayden, Tom, 56
Hayes, Alfred, 65
Hays, Charles, 32
Hearst, William Randolph, 48, 51
Henie, Sonja, 48
Hergetts Company, H., 55
Hill, Phil, 49
Hippodrome Carousel, 46, *83*
Holt, D.G., 70
Homelessness, 80
Hopkins, Mark, 27
Horatio West Court, 66
Horseshoe Pier, 45
Hospitals, 60, *60*, 61, 71, *71*
Hotels, 15, *16-17* 18, *26-27*, 35, 60, 61, 62-63, 67, 79, 80
Howell, E.P., 63
Hromadka, August, 21, 60-61
Hromadka, John, 60, 61
Hueneme & Malibu & Port Los Angeles Railroad, 92
Hughes, Howard, 68
Huntington, Collis P., 27, 28, 29-30, 31, 32, 33, 35

Immanuel Methodist Episcopal Church, 67
Ince, Thomas, 44, *96*, 97
Inceville, 44, *96*, 97
Indians, 10, 11-12, 13, 89
Isherwood, Christopher, 49

Jail, 55
Jefferson School, 64
Jones, George Merritt, 45
Jones, Georgina, 17, *20*
Jones house, Roy, 66
Jones, John P., 18, 19, *19*, 20, 25, 26, 27-28, 31, 32, 38, 44, 51, 62, 70, 71
Jones, Marion, *20*, 39
Jones pier, 45
Jones, Robert F., 23

Kalem movie studio, 41
Keller, Henry, 91
Keller, Mateo (Matthew), 90, 91
Keller's Shelter, 97
Kibben, George, 57
King, Maurice, 57
Kinney, Abbot, 38, 44-45, 67, 73, 74, *74*, 76, 78, *78*, 79; home of, *78*
Kinney, Helen, *78*
Kinney, Thornton, *78*
Kinney, Winifred, *78*
Kowalsky, Henry, 67

Ladd, A.E., 54, 55
La Monica Ballroom, 46, *45*, *47*, 50
Land auctions, 18-19, *22*, 23, *28*
Land grants, 12-13, 90
Lear, William P., 49
LeMay, Curtis, 68
Lennon sisters, 48
LeRoy, Mervyn, 49
Lesser, Sol, 45
Lewis, Thomas A., 56
Libraries, 67-68, 71, 91, *133*
Lick Pier, James, 46, 50
Light rail, 35
Lincoln High School, 63, 64
Lincoln Park, 39
Lindbergh, Charles, *49*
Loamshire Hotel, 61
Long Wharf, 30, 31, *31*, 32-33, *32*
Looff, Charles, 46
Looff Pleasure Pier, *44-45*
Loomis, M.L., 61
Loos, Anita, 49
Lorings Lunch Room, *46*
Los Angeles & Independence Railroad, 23, 26-28, 29, 33, 37, 44
Los Angeles & San Pedro Railroad, 91
Los Angeles Athletic Club, 37
Los Angeles Examiner, 95
Los Angeles Express, 31
Los Angeles Herald, 31
Los Angeles Pacific railway, 33, *34*
Los Angeles Terminal Railroad, 29
Los Angeles Times, 31, 95
Lucas rancho, 20
Lugo, Jose, 14
Lutheran Hospital Society, 61
Lyman, Abe, 50

McCarey, Leo, 49
McClure Tunnel, Robert E., 35
McDonnell Aircraft, 68
McElroy, W.E., 97
Machado, Augustin, 12, 13
Machado family, 15
Machado, Frank, *38*
Machado, Ignacio, 13
McKinne, F.C., 54
McKusick, H.P., 61
McPherson, Aimee Semple, 80
Maharishi Mahesh Yogi, 97
Malibu, 89-93
Malibu Colony, 93, 97
Malibu Park Junior High, 65
Malibu Ranch, 91, 92, 93, 97
Marblehead Land Company, 93
Marina del Rey, 29
Marine Street Telephone Exchange, 80
Marquez, Bonifacio, *11*
Marquez family, *12*, 15, 16; and botulism, 21, 60; cemetery of, 97
Marquez, Francisco, 12, 21
Marquez, Pascual, 21, 44; bathhouse of, *42*
Marsh, Norman, 78
Masonic Hall, 67
Mayer, Louis B., 49
Mendotta Block, 80
Mendoza, Antonio de, 10
Merchants National Bank, 21
Methodist Episcopal Church, 64, 65, 66, 71; Pacific Coast Chautauqua Camp, *92*; Southern Califor-

nia Conference, 94
Metropolitan Water District, 59
Mexican-American War, 14, 21
Miles Playhouse, 66
Million Dollar Pier, *44*, 45
Miramar, *20*, 20
Miramar Beach Club, *40*
Miramar Hotel, *20*, 20, *40*
Miramar Moreton Bay Fig Tree, 66
Mission system, 10
Moon, Michael, 57
Morahan, Eugene, 23
Moran, Gertrude, 39
Moran House, 51, 66
Morgan, Julia, 51
Morongo House, 18
Mortensen, Florence, 60
Mortensen, William, 60, 61
Mosse, Elfie, 67
Mountain, Mattie, 65

National Center for Transcendental Meditation, 97
National Home for Disabled Volunteer Soldiers. *See* Soldiers Home
Neilson Way, 80
Newcomb, Enid, 51
Newcomb, Walter, 51
Newmark, Harris, 23, 67
Newspapers, 23, 69-70, 76
Nichiren Shoshusokagakkai Academy, 67
"99 Steps," *8*, 44, *54*, 96
Norman, Merle, 49
Norman Pavilion, Merle, 61
North Beach Bath House, *38*, *42*, *43*, 44
Noyes, E.W., 23

Ocean Park, 45, 57, 63, 73-74, *75*, 76, *78*; post office, 76
Ocean Park Bank, *75*
Ocean Park Bath House, *43*
Ocean Park Boulevard, *87*
Ocean Park Library, 66, 67-68
Ocean Park Piers, 46, 51, *74-75*, 77, 80
Ocean Park Review, 76
Ocean Skywayride, *46*
Ocean View Hotel, 80
Oil boom, 80
Olewine, Ted, 39
Olivera, Angie Marquez, 21
Olsen, Robert E., 49
Omarr, Sydney, 49
Outlook, The, 23, 31, 67, 69-70

Pacific Coast Chautauqua Camp, *92*, 94
Pacific Coast Highway, 30, *88*
Pacific Electric railway, 33, 35
Pacific Ocean Park, 46, 51
Pacific Palisades, *94*, 94-97
Palisades Park, 23, *84-85*
Parkhurst Building, 66
Parkinson Home, 66
Pasadena & Pacific Railway, *24*, 33
Pavilion Restaurant, 44
Phillips Chapel, 65
Pickering, Ernest, 51
Pickering Pier, 45
Pickford, Mary, *48*
Pico, Andreas, 14
Pico family, 14
Pico, Pio, 13

135

Pier Avenue, 75
Pier Preservation Ordinance, 51
Piers, 44-45, 44, 44-45, 46, 51
Pilgrim Lutheran Church, 65
Pioneer Oil Company, 91
Police department, 57-58, 57
Port Los Angeles, 30, 31, 32, 33
Portola, Gaspar de, 10-11, 90
Port status, fight for, 26-33
Presbyterians, 65
Proposition One, 51
Prospect Hill, 64
Prudhomme, Leon, 90
Puritas, 59, 60

Railroads, 23, 25-27, 28, 29, 30, 32, 33, 34, 37, 91, 92; trains, 30, 31; accident, 33
Ramish, Adolph, 45
Rancho Cucamonga, 90
Ranchos, 12-14, 15, 16, 18
Randall, Ellis, 58
Rapp Saloon, 41, 66, 71
Reagan, Ronald, 49, 97
Recreation, 15, 38-39, 45, 80
Rent control, 56
Rex (gambling ship), 39
Reyes family, 12, 15, 16
Reyes, Herminia, 13
Reyes, Ysidro, 12
Rhodes, Thomas, 56
Rindge, Frederick H., 41, 91, 92
Rindge, Rhoda May Knight, 91, 92-93
Riviera Polo Club, 39
Roach, Hal, 49, 68
Rogers, Will, 39, 49, 49; home, 97; monument, 51
Rogers School, Will, 64
Roller coasters, 34-35, 45, 46
Roosevelt Highway, 30
Rosemary theater, 45
Russell, C.H., 78
Rustic Canyon, 91, 92
Ryan, Elizabeth, 39
Ryan, Francis, 45, 73, 74

St. Anne's Church, 65
Saint Augustine, 11
St. Augustine by-the-Sea Episcopal Church, 14, 65
St. Catherine's Hospital, 61
St. Clement's Church, 65
St. John's Hospital and Health Center, 61, 71
St. Mark's Hotel, 79
Saint Monica, 11; statue of, 23
St. Monica's Church, 65
Saloons, 39, 41, 41
Sand and Sea Club, 51
San Mateo (steamer), 32
San Pedro, 26, 29, 30-31, 32
Santa Fe Railroad. *See* Atchison, Topeka & Santa Fe
Santa Monica Airport, 65, 66, 68-69
Santa Monica Alternative School, 63
Santa Monica Bank, 61
Santa Monica Bathhouse, 44
Santa Monica Bay, 26, 39
Santa Monica Board of Trustees, 54
Santa Monica Canyon, 14, 15, 62, 63, 96
Santa Monica city government, 54-57
Santa Monica City Hall, 67, 70, 71, 91
Santa Monica Civic Auditorium, 57
Santa Monica College, 65

Santa Monica Commercial Company, 20-21
Santa Monica Depot, 30
Santa Monica Designated Landmarks, 66
Santa Monica Free Methodist Church, 65
Santa Monica High School, 64
Santa Monica Hose and Hook and Ladder Company, 58-59
Santa Monica Hospital, 60, 61, 71
Santa Monica Hotel, 16-17, 26-27, 62-63
Santa Monica Improvement Club, 38
Santa Monica incorporation: as a town, 18; as a city, 41, 53, 54
Santa Monica Junior College, 64
Santa Monica Land and Water Company, 23, 71, 93
Santa Monica Medical Center, 61
Santa Monicans for Renters Rights, 56
Santa Monica Place, 87
Santa Monica Pleasure Pier, 45, 46, 47, 51, 51, 66, 82-83, 83
Santa Monica Savings Bank, 61
Santa Monica Technical School, 64-65
Santa Monica Wharf, 29
San Vicente y Santa Monica rancho, 12-13, 15, 16
Schader Real Estate promotion, 22
Schenick, Joseph, 49
Schools, 52, 54, 55, 61-65, 62, 63
Seaside Hotel, 18
Self-Realization Fellowship, 67, 97
Selznick, David O., 49
Sepulveda Adobe, 10-11
Sepulveda family, 14
Sepulveda, Fernando, 12, 13, 14, 15, 16
Sepulveda, Jose, 14, 16
Sepulveda, Ramona, 13
Serra Retreat, 97
Seventh Day Adventist Church, 65
Shearer, Derek, 56
Sherman, Moses H., 33, 74
Shoo Fly Landing, 15-16, 26, 27, 44
Sikking, Sue, 67
Sisters of Charity of Leavenworth, 61
Sisters of the Holy Name, 65
Sixth Street School, 52, 62, 63
Smith, A.J., 57
Soldiers Home, 20, 33, 65, 70-71, 70; trolley station, 35
Southern California Lawn Tennis Association, 38
Southern Pacific Railroad, 27, 28, 29, 30, 31, 32, 33, 37; accident, 33; depot, 26-27; trains, 30, 31
South Loop, 74, 76
South Santa Monica Sunday School, 65
Spanish expeditions, 10-11, 89-90
Stanford, Leland, 27, 29
State Highway 1, 92
Steamers, 32, 29, 38
Stearns, Abel, 18
Stearns, Arcadia Bandini de. *See* Baker, Arcadia Bandini Stearns de
Steere, John, 54, 55
Streetcars. *See* Trolleys
Subway, 35
Sunset Memorial Seat, 51
Sunset Trail, 18-19
Sutton, May, 39

Talamantes, Felipe, 13
Talamantes, Tomas, 13
Tapia, Jose Bartolemeo, 90
Tapia, Maria, 90

Tapia, Tiburcio, 90
Temescal Canyon, 95
Temple, Shirley, 48, 48
Terminal Island, 29
Thalberg, Irving, 49
Timm's Landing, 26
Topanga Canyon, 92
Tourism, 15, 37-38
Trinity Baptist Church, 65
Trinity Mission, 65
Trolleys, 24, 33-34, 34, 53-54, 74, 76
Truxton, 18
Tunney, John, 49
Turpin, Ben, 44
Tynan, Ed, 55

Unitarian Church, 67
Unity By The Sea church, 67
Uplifters Club, 39, 94-95

Valentine, Frederick, 92
Vanderbilt Cup, 39
Vawter, Edwin James, 20-21
Vawter family, 65
Vawter, William S., 20-21, 53-54, 54, 56, 74
Vawter, Williamson D., 20
Venice, 72, 74, 76, 78-80, 78-79, 79, 85
Venice Short Line, 33
Venice Pier, 45, 59, 79; auditorium, 76
Veterans Administration, 69. *See also* Soldiers Home
Veterans Hospital, 33
Vigilance Committee, 90
Villa Aurora, 49
Vitagraph movie studio, 41, 41
Vizcaino, Sebastian, 11, 89-90

Wadsworth Hospital, 71
Walker Board, 32
Warner, Harry, 49
Warren, Earl, 39
Washington School, 63
Water management, 59, 79
Waterman, Waldo, 49
Welk, Lawrence, 48, 50
Westside Council of Churches, 67
Westside Ecumenical Conference, 67
Wharves, 15-16, 29, 30, 31, 31, 32, 44
Whiteman, Paul, 50
Whitton, Alice, 62
Wicks, Moses, 29
Williams, J.H.P., 62-63
Wilshire Palisades Building, 51
Wolfskill family, 70, 71
Women's Christian Temperance Union, 67
Woodlawn Cemetery, 21
Woodward, Ellis, 70
World War II, 34, 50
Wyler, William, 68

Yoganda, Parmahansa, 97
YMCA, 74

Zanuck, Darryl, 4